Beauty and the Beast
La Bella y la Bestia

Codeswitch castellano english
Texto bilingüe

Libro 4

Geoff Willis

Copyright © 2023 Geoff Willis

All rights reserved.

No portion of this book, including illustrations, may be reproduced, copied, distributed or adapted in any way, with the exception of certain activities permitted by applicable copyright laws.

Illustrations were created by Wafflecaramel, illustrations are the property of Geoff Willis, and are subject to copyright.

Reservados todos los derechos

Ninguna parte de este libro, incluidas las ilustraciones, puede reproducirse, copiarse, distribuirse o adaptarse de ninguna manera, con la excepción de ciertas actividades permitidas por las leyes de derechos de autor aplicables.

Ilustraciones creadas por Wafflecaramel, las ilustraciones son propiedad de Geoff Willis y están sujetas a derechos de autor.

Geoff Willis has asserted his right under the Copyright, Designs and Patents Act, 1988, to be identified as the author of this work.

ISBN: 978-1-916738-07-2

Ilustración de portada y frontispicio de Wafflecaramel

ÍNDICE

A	Introducción	1
B	La Bella y la Bestia - Castellano	6
C	Beauty and the Beast – Spanish to English	18
D	Notas Finales	64
E	Un poco de gramática – Verbos compuestos	65
F	Palabras - Ordenado por Sección	87
G	Palabras - Orden Alfabético	97

Beauty and the Beast

A
Introducción

A.1 Objetivo

Este libro es el cuarto de una serie de libros de lectura en inglés.

Estos han sido diseñados para mejorar rápidamente tu capacidad de leer en inglés, y que puedas leer textos básicos sin necesidad de usar un diccionario o un libro de gramática.

Los libros *Codeswitch* están diseñados para ser leídos en orden. Este libro está pensado para quienes han leído y comprendido, al menos en lo esencial, el libro 3, *Little Red Riding Hood*.

Aprender un nuevo idioma es difícil por dos razones. En primer lugar, la gramática del nuevo idioma es diferente a la de tu propio idioma. En segundo lugar, porque necesitas aprender muchas palabras nuevas.

Los libros *Codeswitch* facilitan el aprendizaje del inglés al copiar cómo los niños aprenden sus propios idiomas.

La historia de este libro usa gramática inglesa completa desde la primera oración, pero el vocabulario comienza casi completamente en castellano.

Luego, se introducen a la vez unas pocas palabras en inglés, de modo que estas puedan entenderse fácilmente en el contexto de las palabras circundantes que hay en castellano.

De esta forma, tanto la gramática como el vocabulario del inglés se pueden aprender de manera intuitiva; absorbido por ósmosis. Para introducir las nuevas palabras lentamente, las historias se repiten varias veces. Esto también permite la repetición de palabras que sólo se usan una vez en la historia.

A.2 Antecedentes

He llamado a estos libros *Codeswitch* Castellano *English* por un tipo de lenguaje común que se encuentra entre los hablantes bilingües. En *Codeswitch*, «*code*» se usa para significar «idioma», y «*switch*» significa cambiar repentinamente. Entonces, un lenguaje *Codeswitch* es aquel en el que las personas intercambian rápidamente dos idiomas diferentes.

Este libro comienza como un lenguaje *Codeswitch*. Comienza con gramática inglesa y palabras en castellano y te permite cambiar lentamente y, con suerte, sin dolor, del castellano al inglés.

A.3 Estructura

La sección B de este libro es una traducción completa al castellano de *La bella y la bestia*. Puedes leerla primero si no recuerdas la historia. También puedes usar esta versión para comparar la gramática inglesa de la sección C con la gramática del castellano.

Para introducir todas las palabras necesarias en inglés, unas pocas a la vez, la sección C tiene seis versiones mixtas en castellano/inglés. El nivel C.4, que es el último, está escrito en inglés.

Al final del libro he enumerado todo el vocabulario dos veces. Primero, en el orden en que se introducen las palabras, y después, en el orden alfabético de las palabras en inglés.

Las listas de palabras no pretenden ser diccionarios adecuados. Normalmente sólo coloco una traducción simple al castellano. A veces, he intentado capturar palabras con alternativas comunes, especialmente cuando se usa un significado secundario en la historia.

Lo más importante que debes recordar al leer este libro es que todas las historias, desde la primera palabra de la sección C.1, están escritas en gramática inglesa. Esto es cierto y especialmente confuso con el nivel C.1 de este libro, donde muchas de las palabras son en castellano.

A.4 Cómo usar este libro

Cada una de las historias contadas en estos libros se divide en secciones de aproximadamente doscientas palabras cada una.

En cada sección se introduce un promedio de unas cinco palabras nuevas en inglés. El número real de palabras varía, a veces se introducen hasta doce palabras, pero otras veces no se introduce ninguna palabra nueva.

La mejor manera de leer estos libros es mantener la lectura a un nivel cómodo y agradable, repitiendo la lectura.

Entonces, comienza desde el principio y empieza a leer el nivel C.1.01 de este libro. Mientras puedas entender fácilmente la historia, continúa leyendo.

Sigue leyendo hasta que haya demasiadas palabras nuevas y tengas dificultades para comprender lo que sucede en la historia.

Tan pronto como se torne un poco difícil, vuelve a un nivel más fácil.

Te recomiendo retroceder mucho, al menos seis tramos, aunque lo ideal sería retroceder uno o dos niveles. De modo que, si estás a la mitad del nivel C.3 y las cosas se ponen difíciles, regresa al comienzo del nivel C.2 de ese libro.

Si te resulta difícil leer este libro y estás tratando de solucionar las cosas, entonces ya no estás aprendiendo inglés como lo hace un niño.

En este punto, es mejor volver a un lugar del libro donde la lectura sea muy fácil y seguir adelante. Cada vez que hagas esto, verás que avanzas más antes de que el libro se vuelva difícil nuevamente.

A.5 Un poco de gramática

En comparación con la mayoría de los idiomas, el inglés tiene una gramática muy simple, generalmente más simple que la del castellano.

Además, la gramática del inglés y la del castellano son muy similares.

He incluido un poco de gramática en la sección E de cada uno de estos libros. Sin embargo, esto se limita principalmente a áreas donde el inglés es significativamente diferente al castellano.

El libro 1 trataba de sustantivos, el libro 2 analizaba los verbos estándar, el libro 3 analizaba los verbos auxiliares, y este libro analiza los verbos compuestos.

Estas secciones de gramática no son esenciales, si prefieres, puedes pasar directamente al libro 5 después de leer la sección D.

A.5.1 Palabras confusas

Las palabras de la tabla A.5.1 a continuación tienen la misma ortografía en castellano y en inglés, pero tienen significados diferentes.

En este libro sólo se usan las versiones en inglés, nunca se usan las del castellano.

Beauty and the Beast

Tabla A.5.1			
Palabra en los libros	Pronunciación inglesa	En las historias, significa	En las historias, nunca significa
a	a /ə/	un, uno, una	en una dirección
alas	alás /əlás/	¡ay! ¡caramba!	extremidad de un pájaro
come	cum /kəm/	venga, viene	consumir comida
has	has (con «h» no silente)	tiene / ha	segunda persona presente de hacer
he	hii (con «h» no silente)	él	primera persona presente de hacer
once	hü-uns (con «h» silente)	una vez	11
pan	pan	sartén	un bocadillo
use	ius	presente de usar	subjuntivo de usar
vine	vain	vid, planta trepadora, planta enredadera	pretérito perfecto de venir

A.5.2 Palabras con apóstrofos

Las palabras en inglés a veces tienen apóstrofos.

En ocasiones esto se debe a que las palabras están contraídas, y otras a que son posesivas.

Todos los ejemplos del uso del apóstrofo introducido en este libro se muestran en la tabla A.5.2 a continuación:

Tabla A.5.2		
Contracción	Forma completa	Significado en este libro
beast's	posesivo 1.E.3	de la bestia
beauty's	posesivo 1.E.3	de la bella
father's	posesivo 1.E.3	del padre

B

La Bella y la Bestia - Castellano

B.01

Había una vez un comerciante que tenía tres hijas. Las dos mayores eran bastante bonitas, pero la tercera era una belleza, y no se equivocaba. Sus ojos eran tan azules como el cielo, su cabello era tan negro como el ébano y sus mejillas eran como rosas. El comerciante amaba mucho a sus dos hijas mayores, pero amaba aún más a Bella.

Las cosas fueron agradables durante mucho tiempo, y el comerciante era rico y próspero, pero luego las cosas empezaron a ir mal para él. Uno tras otro, sus barcos se perdieron en el mar y gran parte de su fortuna se perdió con ellos.

Entonces, un día, el comerciante llamó a sus hijas y les dijo: "Hijas mías, necesito hacer un largo viaje. Ya no soy un hombre rico, pero deseo traer a casa un regalo para cada uno de ustedes, así que díganme qué les gustaría tener".

Las dos hijas mayores comenzaron a pensar en todas las cosas que querían, y cada una temía que la otra obtuviera algo mejor que ella.

B.02

Por fin, la mayor habló, "Querido padre", dijo ella, "Ojalá me trajeras una túnica de terciopelo bordada en oro, zapatos a juego y un abanico para agitar en la mano".

"Y yo", dijo la segunda, "quisiera un collar de perlas, y perlas para mi cabello, y un brazalete fino".

Al comerciante le preocupaba que sus hijas pidieran cosas tan caras, pero no le gustaba rechazarlas.

"Y tú, Bella", dijo, volviéndose hacia su hija menor, "¿qué te gustaría?"

"Querido padre", dijo, "me has dado tanto que no me queda nada que desear; pero si me traes algo, que sea una rosa ".

Cuando sus hermanas mayores escucharon esto, se enojaron mucho. Pensaban que Bella sólo había pedido una rosa para avergonzarlos delante de su padre y hacerle pensar que era menos egoísta que ellos. Pero Bella no había tenido ese pensamiento.

El comerciante sonrió a su hija menor y la besó tres veces, pero solo besó a sus hijas mayores una vez. Luego se montó en su caballo y se alejó.

B.03

Continuó viajando durante varios días y finalmente llegó a la ciudad a la que se dirigía. Allí descubrió que había perdido aún más fortuna de lo que pensaba. Ahora era un hombre pobre.

Aún así, logró comprar los regalos que le habían pedido sus dos hijas mayores, y luego, con el corazón triste, se dirigió a casa.

Sin embargo, no había viajado mucho cuando fue alcanzado por una tormenta y se perdió en un bosque profundo. Cabalgó de un lado a otro, tratando de encontrar la salida, y de repente llegó a un lugar abierto, y allí vio un magnífico castillo frente a él.

El comerciante estaba asombrado. Nunca había oído hablar de un castillo así en ese bosque. Cabalgó hasta la puerta y llamó, esperando encontrar refugio para pasar la noche.

Tan pronto como llamó a la gran puerta, esta se abrió frente a él. Entró y miró a su alrededor, no había nadie; todo estaba en silencioso.

B.04

Pasó de una habitación a otra. Todo era magnífico y bien arreglado, pero no se veía ni un alma. Por fin llegó a una habitación donde estaba preparada la cena. Los platos eran todos de oro, y las carnes y frutas eran de las más raras y deliciosas.

El comerciante estaba tan hambriento que se sentó a la mesa, y de inmediato la comida le fue servida por manos invisibles, mientras una música suave sonaba desde una habitación escondida más allá.

Comió bien y luego se levantó y fue a buscar un lugar para dormir. Pronto encontró un lugar. Habían preparado una cama en una habitación grande, y allí se desvistió y, acostado, durmió hasta la mañana sin que lo molestaran.

Cuando se despertó, descubrió que le habían quitado su propia ropa sucia. En su lugar se había colocado un hermoso traje, del tipo más lujoso. También había una bolsa llena de piezas de oro. Preguntándose aún más, el comerciante se levantó, se vistió y salió a los jardines a mirar a su alrededor.

B.05

Aquí todo era más hermoso que cualquier jardín que hubiera visto antes. Había caminos sinuosos y fuentes, árboles frutales y plantas con flores.

Junto a una de las fuentes había un rosal cubierto de rosas. La vista de las rosas le recordó al comerciante el deseo de Bella, y pensó que no haría ningún daño romper una para llevársela. Eligió la rosa más grande y fina. Pero, en el momento en que la arrancó, el aire se llenó con el sonido de un trueno, el suelo se meció bajo sus pies y una bestia de aspecto terrible apareció frente a él.

"¡Hombre miserable!" gritó la Bestia, "¿qué has hecho? Te ofrecieron todo lo mejor del castillo. ¿Por qué has roto mi rosal que es más querido para mí que nada en el mundo? Ahora por esto seguramente debes morir ".

El comerciante estaba aterrorizado.

"¡Oh, querida, buena Bestia, por favor no me mates!" gritó. "No quise hacer daño. Por favor, déjame ir y no volveré a molestarte ".

"No, no", respondió la Bestia. "No escaparás tan fácilmente. Has roto mi rosal y debes sufrir por ello."

B.06

Sin embargo, el comerciante suplicó y suplicó que se le perdonara y, por fin, la Bestia se apiadó de él. "Si te perdono la vida", dijo, "¿qué me darás a cambio?"

"Ay," dijo el comerciante, "¿qué puedo darte? He perdido toda mi fortuna y ahora soy un hombre pobre. No me queda nada en el mundo más que mis tres hijas ".

"Dame una de tus hijas por esposa y estaré satisfecho", dijo la Bestia.

El comerciante se horrorizó ante la idea de tal cosa. Quería negarse, pero tenía miedo de que si lo hacía, la Bestia lo haría pedazos.

"Puedes tener tres meses para pensarlo", dijo la Bestia. "Pero debes prometerme que al final de ese tiempo regresarás aquí y me traerás una de tus hijas o vendrás preparado para morir".

El comerciante se vió obligado a prometer esto; no pudo evitarlo. Tan pronto como prometió, la Bestia desapareció y el hombre quedó libre para irse, por lo que se fue rápidamente.

B.07

Cabalgó hacia su casa, pero el corazón le oprimía el pecho. No veía cómo podía dar a una de sus hijas para que fuera la esposa de una horrible bestia y, sin embargo, no quería morir.

Sus hijas lo recibieron con alegría, y las dos hermanas mayores se alegraron al ver los hermosos obsequios que les había traído. Solo Bella notó su mirada triste y abatida.

"Querido padre", dijo ella, "¿por qué estás preocupado? ¿Te ha pasado algo malo?

Al principio su padre no quiso decírselo, pero ella le instó y le suplicó que se lo dijera hasta que finalmente él no pudo seguir callado. Les contó a sus hijas todo sobre el castillo y lo que sucedió allí, y sobre la Bestia, y cómo, a menos que una de ellas accediera a casarse con la Bestia, tendría que perder la vida.

Cuando las hijas mayores escucharon esto, casi se desmayaron. Incluso para salvar la vida de su padre, no podían acceder a casarse con una criatura así.

"Querido padre", dijo Bella, "no morirás. Seré la novia de la Bestia".

"Sí, sí", gritaron sus hermanas. "Eso es correcto. Si Bella no hubiera pedido la rosa, este problema no habría sucedido ".

B.08

Al principio, el comerciante no estaba de acuerdo con esto. Bella era la más querida para él de todas sus hijas. Tenía la esperanza de que si alguna de ellas se casaba con la Bestia, sería una de las hermanas mayores. Pero no quisieron oír hablar de esto y cuando, al cabo de tres meses, el comerciante se dispuso a regresar al castillo, se llevó a Bella con él.

Cabalgaron y cabalgaron y después de un tiempo llegaron al bosque, y el comerciante no tardó mucho en encontrar el castillo. Llamó a la puerta, y se abrió como antes, y él y Bella entraron de una habitación a otra, y todo era tan magnífico que ella tuvo que admirarlo. Por fin llegaron al comedor y allí se les preparó un delicioso banquete.

Se sentaron y comieron mientras sonaba una música suave a su alrededor. Bella empezó a pensar que el dueño de todo esto no podía ser una criatura tan terrible después de todo.

B.09

Pero tan pronto como terminaron de cenar, la Bestia apareció frente a ellos, y cuando Bella lo vio comenzó a temblar y temblar, porque tenía un aspecto aún más terrible de lo que su padre había dicho.

"No me tengas miedo, Bella", dijo con voz suave. "No te haré daño. Tu padre te ha traído aquí, y es cierto que debes quedarte aquí, pero no tienes que casarte conmigo a menos que estés segura de que estás dispuesta a hacerlo ".

"No quiero casarme contigo, Bestia, y debes saberlo", dijo Bella.

"Pero tengo miedo de que si no me caso contigo, harás daño a mi padre".

"No, Bella, no le haré daño. Él puede irse en paz, y tal vez después de que hayas estado aquí un tiempo, puedas aprender a quererme lo suficiente como para que te casas conmigo ".

Bella no lo creía, pero la Bestia hablaba con tanta dulzura que ya no le temía, y cuando llegó el momento de que su padre se fuera, se despidió de él y no lo entristeció con lágrimas.

B.10

Después de eso, Bella vivió allí en el castillo de la Bestia y estaba contenta. Todos los días ella salía a los jardines, y la Bestia venía y jugaba con ella un rato, y ella se encariñó mucho con él. Todos los días, antes de dejarla, le decía: "Bella, ¿estás dispuesta a casarte conmigo?".

Pero Bella siempre respondió,

"No, querida Bestia, no deseo casarme contigo."

Entonces la Bestia suspiraría profundamente y se alejaría.

Un día, Bella estaba sentada frente a un gran espejo en su habitación y estaba triste porque no había visto a su padre durante tanto tiempo.

"Ojalá", dijo ella, "pudiera ver lo que mi querido padre está haciendo en este mismo momento".

Mientras decía esto, levantó los ojos hacia el espejo. Se sorprendió mucho al ver en el espejo el reflejo de una habitación completamente diferente a la que ella estaba. Era una habitación de su propia casa la que vio reflejada allí. Vio en él las imágenes de su padre y sus hermanas. Podía verlos sonreír y moverse, y podía decir exactamente lo que estaban haciendo. Descubrió que podía mirarlos en el espejo todo el tiempo que quisiera y cuando quisiera.

B.11

Después de esto, Bella solía sentarse frente al espejo, y solo tenía que desearlo y podía ver su casa y todo lo que estaba sucediendo allí.

Pero un día, cuando se sentó frente al espejo, vio que su padre estaba enfermo. Estaba acostado en su cama tan pálido y débil que Bella estaba aterrorizada. Se levantó de un salto y salió corriendo al jardín llamando a la Bestia.

De inmediato apareció frente a ella. "¿Qué es?" preguntó la Bestia con ansiedad. "¿Qué te ha asustado, Bella?"

"¡Ay!", Gritó, "mi padre está enfermo. Oh, querida y amable Bestia, por favor déjame ir con él y te amaré para siempre ".

La Bestia parecía muy seria.

"Muy bien, Bella", dijo, "te dejaré ir, porque no puedo negarte nada. Pero prométeme que volverás al cabo de una semana, porque si no lo haces, me sucederá una gran desgracia ".

B.12

Bella estaba muy dispuesta a prometer esto. La Bestia luego le dio un anillo con un gran rubí. "Cuando te vayas a la cama esta noche", dijo, "gira el rubí hacia la palma de tu mano y desearás estar en la casa de tu padre, y por la mañana te darás cuenta de que estás allí. Cuando estas lista para regresar, haga lo mismo y se encontrará nuevamente en el castillo.

Pero no olvides que al cabo de una semana, a la hora exacta, debes regresar o me traerás sufrimiento ".

Bella hizo lo que la Bestia le dijo. Esa noche, cuando se acostó, giró el rubí del anillo hacia la palma de su mano y deseó estar en la casa de su padre. Estaba muy feliz cuando se despertó a la mañana siguiente y se encontró en su propia cama en casa. Se levantó y corrió a la habitación de su padre, y el comerciante se alegró tanto de verla que, a partir de esa hora, empezó a mejorar, y a los pocos días estaba tan bien como siempre.

B.13

Las hermanas de Bella le hicieron muchas preguntas sobre el castillo donde vivía, y cuando se enteraron de lo bonito que era y de lo feliz que estaba allí, se llenaron de envidia.

"Bella siempre consigue lo mejor de todo", se decían la una a la otra. "Es más joven que cualquiera de nosotros, pero mira lo bien que vive; mucho mejor que nosotros ".

Luego planearon juntas cómo podrían evitar que Bella regresara al castillo al final de la semana.

"Si tan solo pudieramos hacer que ella rompa su promesa a la Bestia", dijeron, "él podría enojarse tanto con ella que la enviariá lejos y se llevariá a uno de nosotros a vivir en su castillo".

El día antes de que Bella regresara con la Bestia, pusieron un poco de polvos para dormir en la copa de la que bebió.

Tan pronto como Bella hubo tragado el polvo, sintió mucho sueño. Sus párpados pesaban como plomo, y pronto cayó en un sueño profundo, y no se despertó durante dos días y dos noches.

B.14

Al final de ese tiempo, Bella tuvo un sueño, y en su sueño caminó por los jardines del castillo. Llegó al rosal junto a la fuente, y allí yacía la pobre Bestia tendida en el suelo, y estaba casi muerto. Abrió los ojos y la miró con tristeza.

"Ah, Bella, Bella", dijo, "¿por qué rompiste tu promesa de regresar al cabo de una semana? Mira el sufrimiento que me has traído ".

Bella se despertó sollozando amargamente.

"¡Ay, ay!" ella lloró. "Debo irme de inmediato. Siento que le ha ocurrido algo a la Bestia, y que es mi culpa, aunque no sé cómo. " No se dio cuenta de que había estado dormida durante dos días y dos noches.

Giró el anillo de rubí con el rubí hacia la palma de su mano, deseó regresar al castillo y luego se acostó y se fue a dormir.

B.15

Cuando se despertó, estaba de nuevo en el castillo y era temprano en la mañana. Salió corriendo al jardín y se dirigió directamente al rosal. Allí, como en su sueño, vio a la Bestia tendida en el suelo, y parecía estar sin vida y sin aliento. Bella se tiró al suelo y tomó su cabeza en su regazo, y sus lágrimas corrieron y cayeron sobre él, y le pareció que ni siquiera amaba a su padre tanto como amaba a la Bestia.

"Oh, Bestia, querida, querida Bestia", gritó, "¿puedes oírme? ¿Estás realmente muerto?

Entonces la Bestia abrió los ojos y la miró.

"Ah, Bella", dijo, "pensé que me habías abandonado. ¿Todavía no me amas lo suficiente como para casarte conmigo?

"¡Oh, sí! Te amo lo suficiente y con mucho gusto seré tu esposa ", exclamó Bella.

Tan pronto como ella dijo esto, la piel áspera y peluda de la Bestia se desmoronó, y un apuesto joven príncipe, vestido de satén blanco y plateado se paró frente a ella. Bella lo miró asombrada.

B.16

"Sí, ciertamente serás mi querida esposa", gritó el príncipe, "porque tú y solo tú has roto el hechizo que me tenía".

Entonces el Príncipe, que ya no era una Bestia, le dijo a Bella que un hada malvada lo había cambiado a la forma de una Bestia, y que hasta que una hermosa doncella pudiera amarlo lo suficiente como para ser su esposa, no se rompería el hechizo.

Pero Bella lo había amado por su bondad y generosidad a pesar de su fea forma, y ahora nunca más el hada malvada podría tener ningún poder sobre él.

Y ahora en todo el castillo se oía el sonido de la vida y las voces, y de gente corriendo de un lado a otro. Porque el mismo hechizo que había convertido al Príncipe en una Bestia había hecho a toda su gente invisible, y ahora, ellos también fueron liberados del hechizo.

B.17

Ahora Bella estaba muy feliz. Si había amado a la Bestia, amaba al joven y apuesto príncipe mil veces más. Se preparó un gran banquete de bodas y se envió a buscar a su padre y a sus hermanas. A su padre se le otorgó el lugar de honor, pero fue muy diferente con sus hermanas; debido a la dureza de su corazón, se convirtieron en dos estatuas y se pararon una a cada lado de la puerta.

Beauty and the Beast

Pero Bella era demasiado gentil para enfadarse con ellas. Después de casarse, solía ir y pararse junto a las estatuas y hablar con ellas, y sus lágrimas caían sobre ellas de modo que después de un tiempo sus corazones duros se ablandaban y la piedra volvía a fundirse en carne. Entonces todos fueron muy felices juntos. Las dos hermanas se casaron con dos nobles de la corte.

En cuanto a la Bella y el Príncipe, nada podía igualar el amor que sentían el uno por el otro, y vivieron juntos felices para siempre y no sufrieron más daño.

C
Beauty and the Beast
- Spanish to English

Beauty and the Bestia

C.1.01

There was once a comerciante who had three hijas. The two older ones were pretty enough, but the third was a beauty, and no error. Her eyes were as azul as the cielo, her hair was as negro as ébano, and her cheeks were like roses. The comerciante loved his two older hijas, but he loved Beauty even more apreciadamente.

Things went along agradablemente for a long time, and the comerciante was próspero, but then things began to go wrong for him. One after another, his barcos were perdidos at mar, and a large parte of his fortune was perdido with them.

So, one day, the comerciante called his hijas to him and said, "I need to go on a long viaje. I am no longer a rico man, but I deseo to traer home a regalo for each one of you, so tell me what you would like to have."

The two older hijas began to think of all the things they wanted, and each was temerosa the other would get something better than she did.

C.1.02

At last the first habló, "Dear father," said she, "I deseo you would traer me a terciopelo túnica bordado with gold, and shoes to combinar, and an abanico to ondear in my hand."

"And I," said the second, "would like a necklace of perlas, and perlas for my hair, and a fine pulsera."

The comerciante was preocupado that his hijas should ask for such caro things, but he did not like to refuse them.

"And you, Beauty," he said, turning to his last hija, "what would you like?"

"Dear father," she said, "I have nothing left to desear for; but if you traes me anything at all let it be a rose."

When her older hermanas heard this they were very angry. They thought that Beauty had asked only for a rose so that she would avergonzar them in frente of their father, and make him think she was menos egoísta than they were. But Beauty had had no such thought as that.

The comerciante sonrio at Beauty and besó her three times, but he only besó his older hijas once. Then he got on his caballo and rode away.

Beauty and the Beast

C.1.03

He viajó on for varios days, and at last he reached the ciudad he was going to. Here he descubrió that he had perdido even more of his fortune than he had thought. He was now a pobre man.

Still, he manejó to buy the regalos his two older hijas had asked for, and then with a sad corazón he set out for home.

He had not viajado far, however, when he was superado by a tormenta and got perdido in a profundo forest. He rode this way and that, trying to find the way out, and then suddenly he came to an open place, and there he saw a magnífico castillo in frente of him.

The comerciante was asombrado. He had never heard of such a castillo in that forest. He rode up to the door and knocked, hoping to find refugio for the noche.

As soon as he knocked on the great door, it swung open in frente of him. He went in and looked around, no one was there; everything was silencioso.

C.1.04

He went on into one room after another. Everything was very magnífico and well organizado, but there was not an alma to be seen. At last he came to a room where a cena was set out. The platos were all of gold, deliciosas carnes and frutas.

The comerciante was so hungry that he sat down at the table, and at once the comida was servido to him by invisible hands, while soft música sounded from a hidden room beyond.

He ate well and then got up and went to look for a place to sleep. He soon found a place. A bed had been made ready in a large room, he slept until morning without being perturbado.

When he woke up, he found his own sucio clothes had gone. In their place a bonito traje had been extendido out, of the best kind. There was also a bag lleno with gold pieces. Wondering still more, the comerciante got up and dressed and went out into the jardines to look around.

C.1.05

Here everything was more beautiful than any jardín he had ever seen before. There were serpenteado paths and fuentes, and fruta trees and flowers.

Beside one of the fuentes was a rose arbusto covered with roses. The visión of the roses recordó the comerciante of Beauty's deseo, and he thought it would do no harm to romper off one to take to her. He eligió the largest and best rose. But, the moment he arrancó it, the aire was llenado with a sound of thunder, the suelo rocked under his feet, and a terrible looking beast apareció in frente of him.

"Miserable man!" cried the Beast, "what have you done? All the best in the castillo was ofrecido to you. Why have you broken my rose arbusto that is dearer to me than anything in the world? Now for this you must surely morir."

The comerciante was terrified.

"Oh, dear, good Beast please do not matar me!" he cried. "I meant no harm. Please let me go, and I will never molestar you again."

"No, no," answered the Beast. "You shall not escapar so fácilmente. You have broken my rose-arbusto and you must sufrir for it."

Beauty and the Beast

C.1.06

Still the comerciante rogó and suplicó to be perdonado and at last the Beast had pena on him. "If I perdono your life," he said, "what will you give me in retorno for it?"

"Alas," said the comerciante, "what can I give you? I have perdido all my fortune and I am now a pobre man. I have nothing left in the world but my three hijas."

"Give me one of your hijas for an esposa and I will be satisfecho," said the Beast.

The comerciante was horrorizado at the thought of such a thing. He wanted to refuse, but he was asustado that if he did so, the Beast would tear him to pieces.

"You can have three meses in which to think it over," said the Beast. "But you must promise me that at the end of that time you will regresar here and either traer me one of your hijas or come preparado to morir."

The comerciante was obligado to promise this; he could not ayudar himself. As soon as he had promised the Beast desapareció and the man was libre to go, and so he went quickly.

C.1.07

He rode on toward his home but his corazón was pesado inside his pecho. He did not see how he could posiblemente give one of his hijas to be the novia of an espantoso beast, but also he did not want to morir.

His hijas met him with joy, and the two older hermanas were delighted when they saw the beautiful regalos he had traído them. Only Beauty notó his sad looks.

"Dear father," said she, "why are you preocupado? Has something bad happened to you?"

At first her father would not tell her, but she urgió and rogó him to tell her until finally he could not keep silencio any longer. He told his hijas all about the castillo and what happened there, and of the Beast, and of how unless one of them would consentir to marry the Beast he would have to perdir his life.

When the older hijas heard this they casi desmayaron. Even to salvar their father's life they could not consentir to marry such a criatura.

"Dear father," said Beauty, "you shall not morir. I will be the Beast's novia."

"Yes, yes," cried her hermanas. "That is only right. If Beauty had not asked for the rose this problema would not have happened."

C.1.08

At first the comerciante said no. Beauty was the dearest to him of all his hijas. He had hoped that if any of them was to marry the Beast it might be one of the older hermanas. But they would not escuchar of this and when, at the end of three meses, the comerciante set out to regresar to the castillo he took Beauty with him.

They rode along and rode along and after a while they came to the forest, and it did not take the comerciante long to find the castillo. He knocked on the door, and it opened as before, and he and Beauty went in through one room after another, and everything was so magnífico that she had to admirar it. At last, they came to the dining room, and here a delicioso banquete was set out for them.

They sat down and ate while soft música sounded around them. Beauty began to think the master of all this could not be such a terrible criatura after all.

C.1.09

But as soon as they finished their cena the Beast apareció in frente of them, and when Beauty saw him she began to agitar and tremble, for he was even more terrible looking than her father had said.

"Do not be temerosa of me, Beauty," he said in a suave voice. "I will do you no harm. Your father has traído you here, and it is verdad that you must permanecer here, but you do not have to marry me unless you are sure you are dispuesto to."

"I do not want to marry you, Beast, and you must know that," said Beauty. "But I am asustada that if I do not marry you, you will harm my father."

"No, Beauty, I will not harm him. He may go in peace, and quizás after you have been here a while you may learn to like me enough to marry me."

Beauty did not creer this, but the Beast habló so suavemente that she no longer feared him, and when the time came for her father to go she said goodbye to him and did not sadden him by crying.

C.1.10

After that Beauty lived there in the Beast's castillo and was contenta. Cada day she went out into the jardines, and the Beast came and played with her for a while, and she creció very fond of him. Cada day before he left her he said, "Beauty, are you dispuesto to marry me?"

But Beauty always answered,

"No, dear Beast, I do not desear to marry you."

Then the Beast would suspirar fuertemente and go away.

One day Beauty was sitting in frente of a large espejo in her room, and she was sad because she had not seen her father for so long.

"I deseo," said she, "that I could see what my dear father is doing at this very moment."

As she said this, she elevó her eyes to the espejo. She was very sorprendido to see in the espejo a reflexión of a room completely diferente to the one she was in. It was a room in her own home that she saw reflejada there. She saw in it the imágenes of her father and hermanas. She could see them sonreir and move, and she could tell exactly what they were doing. She found she could watch them in the espejo for as long as she pleased and whenever she pleased.

C.1.11

After this Beauty often came to sit in frente of the espejo, and she only had to desear it and she could see her home, and all that was going on there.

But one day, when she sat down in frente of the espejo, she saw that her father was enfermo. He was lying on his bed so pálido and weak that Beauty was terrified. She jumped up and ran out into the jardín calling for the Beast.

At once he apareció in frente of her. "What is it?" asked the Beast. "What has frightened you, Beauty?"

"Alas," she cried, "my father is enfermo. Oh dear kind Beast, please let me go to him, and I will love you for ever after."

Beauty and the Beast

The Beast looked very grave.

"Very well, Beauty," he said, "I will let you go, for I can refuse you nothing. But promise me you will regresar at the end of a semana, for if you do not some great desgracia will happen to me."

C.1.12

Beauty was very dispuesto to promise this. The Beast then gave her an anillo with a large rubí. "When you go to bed esta noche," he said, "turn the rubí in toward the palma of your hand and desea you were in your father's house, and in the morning, you will find you are there. When you are ready to regresar do the same thing, and you will find that you are back in the castillo again.

But do not forget, that by the end of a semana, to an hour, you must regresar or you will traer sufrimiento upon me."

Beauty did as the Beast told her. That noche when she lay down, she turned the rubí of the anillo in toward the palma of her hand and deseó she was in her father's house. She was very happy, when she woke up the next morning, and found herself in her own bed at home. She got up and ran to her father's room, and the comerciante was so delighted to see her that, from that hour, he began to get better, and in a few days he was as well as ever again.

C.1.13

Beauty's hermanas asked her a lot of preguntas about the castillo where she lived, and when they heard how fine it was, and how happy she was there, they were llenado with envidia.

"Beauty always gets the best of everything," they said to each other. "She is younger than either of nosotros, but look how finely she lives; much better than we do."

Then they planificaron together as to how they could keep Beauty from going back to the castillo at the end of the semana.

"If we can only make her romper her promise to the Beast," they said, "he might be so angry with her that he will send her away and take one of nosotros to live at his castillo instead."

The day before Beauty was due to regresar to the Beast, they put some sleeping powder in the cáliz that she drank from.

As soon as Beauty drank the powder she became very sleepy. Her párpados pesaron like plomo, and soon she fell into a profundo duermevela, and she did not wake up for two days and noches.

C.1.14

At the end of that time Beauty had a dream, and in her dream she walked in the castillo jardines. She came to the rose-arbusto beside the fuente, and there lay the pobre Beast estirado out on the suelo, and he was almost dead. He opened his eyes and looked at her.

"Ah, Beauty, Beauty," he said, "why did you romper your promise to regresar at the end of a semana? See what sufrimiento you have traído on me."

Beauty woke up, crying amargamente.

"Alas, alas!" she cried. "I must go at once. I feel some harm has come to the Beast, and that it is my culpa, though how, I do not know." She did not realise she had been asleep for two days and noches.

She turned the rubí anillo with the rubí toward the palma of her hand, and deseó herself back in the castillo and then lay down and went to sleep.

Beauty and the Beast

C.1.15

When she woke up she was in the castillo again, and it was temprano morning. She ran out into the jardín, and straight to the rose-arbusto. There, as in her dream, she saw the Beast estirado out on the suelo, and he seemed to be without life or respiración. Beauty threw herself down on the suelo and took his head in her regazo, and her tears ran down and fell upon him, and it seemed to her she did not love even her father as apreciadamente as she loved the Beast.

"Oh, Beast - dear, dear Beast," she cried, "can you escuchar me? Are you realmente dead?"

Then the Beast opened his eyes and looked at her.

"Ah, Beauty," he said, "I thought you had deserted me. Do you still not love me enough to marry me?"

"Oh, I do! I do love you enough, and I will be your novia," cried Beauty.

No sooner had she said this than the áspero furry hide of the Beast fell aparte, and a guapo young príncipe, dressed in white satin and silver stood in frente of her. Beauty looked at him in wonder.

C.1.16

"Yes, you shall indeed be my own dear novia," cried the Príncipe, "for you and you solo have broken the hechizo that agarrado me."

Then the Príncipe, a Beast no longer, told Beauty that a malvada hada had cambiado him into the forma of a Beast, and not until a fair young doncella could love him enough to be his novia would the hechizo be broken.

But Beauty had loved him in spite of his fea forma, and now never again could the malvada hada have any poder over him.

And now all through the castillo the sound of life and voices was heard, and of people running to and fro. For the same hechizo that had cambiado the Príncipe to a Beast had made all his people invisible, and now, they too were freed from the hechizo.

C.1.17

Now Beauty was very happy. If she had loved the Beast, she loved the guapo young Príncipe a mil times more. A gran boda banquete was preparado, and her father and hermanas were sent for. Her father had the place of honor, but it was quite diferente with her hermanas; because of their hard corazones they were cambiado into two estatuas and they stood one on either side of the doorway.

But Beauty was too amable to be angry with them. After she was married she often used to go and stand beside the estatuas and talk to them, and her tears fell upon them so that after a while their hard corazones crecieron soft and the stone derretió back to carne again. Then they were all very happy together. The two hermanas married two nobles of the corte.

As for Beauty and the Príncipe, nothing could igual their love for each other, and they lived together happy forever after, and no further harm ever came to them.

Beauty and the Beast

C.2.01

There was once a merchant who had three hijas. The two older ones were pretty enough, but the third was a beauty, and no mistake. Her eyes were as azul as the cielo, her hair was as negro as ébano, and her cheeks were like roses. The merchant loved his two older hijas dearly, but he loved Beauty even more dearly.

Beauty and the Beast

Things went along agradablemente for a long time, and the merchant was rich and próspero, but then things began to go wrong for him. One after another, his ships were lost at sea, and a large parte of his fortune was lost with them.

So, one day, the merchant called his hijas to him and said, "My children, I need to go on a long journey. I am no longer a rich man, but I deseo to traer home a regalo for each one of you, so tell me what you would like to have."

The two older hijas began to think of all the things they wanted, and each was temerosa the other would get something finer than she did.

C.2.02

At last the eldest habló, "Dear father," said she, "I deseo you would traer me a terciopelo robe embroidered with gold, and shoes to match, and an abanico to wave in my hand."

"And I," said the second, "would like a necklace of perlas, and perlas for my hair, and a fine bracelet."

The merchant was preocupado that his hijas should ask for such expensive things, but he did not like to refuse them.

"And you, Beauty," he said, turning to his youngest hija, "what would you like?"

"Dear father," she said, "you have given me so much that I have nothing left to desear for; but if you traes me anything at all let it be a rose."

When her older hermanas heard this they were very angry. They thought that Beauty had asked only for a rose so that she would avergonazar them in frente of their father, and make him think she was less selfish than they were. But Beauty had had no such thought as that.

The merchant sonrio at his youngest hija and besó her three times, but he only besó his older hijas once. Then he got on his horse and rode away.

C.2.03

He viajó on for several days, and at last he reached the city he was going to. Here he descubrió that he had lost even more of his fortune than he had thought. He was now a pobre man.

Still, he manejó to buy the regalos his two older hijas had asked for, and then with a sad corazón he set out for home.

He had not viajó far, however, when he was superado by a storm and got lost in a profundo forest. He rode this way and that, trying to find the way out, and then suddenly he came to an open place, and there he saw a magnífico castillo in frente of him.

The merchant was asombrado. He had never heard of such a castillo in that forest. He rode up to the door and knocked, hoping to find shelter for the noche.

As soon as he knocked on the great door, it swung open in frente of him. He went in and looked around, no one was there; everything was silencioso.

C.2.04

He went on into one room after another. Everything was very magnífico and well arranged, but there was not a soul to be seen. At last he came to a room where a cena was set out. The platos were all of gold, and the meats and frutas were of the rarest and most deliciosas kinds.

Beauty and the Beast

The merchant was so hungry that he sat down at the table, and at once the food was servido to him by invisible hands, while soft música sounded from a hidden room beyond.

He ate well and then got up and went to look for a place to sleep. He soon found a place. A bed had been made ready in a large room, and he undressed there, and, lying down, he slept until morning without being perturbado.

When he woke up, he found his own dirty clothes had been taken away. In their place a bonito suit had been extendido out, of the richest kind. There was also a bag lleno with gold pieces. Wondering still more, the merchant got up and dressed and went out into the jardines to look around.

C.2.05

Here everything was more beautiful than any jardín he had ever seen before. There were winding paths and fuentes, and fruta trees and flowering plantas.

Beside one of the fuentes was a rose arbusto covered with roses. The sight of the roses reminded the merchant of Beauty's deseo, and he thought it would do no harm to romper off one to take to her. He chose the largest and finest rose. But, the moment he arrancó it, the aire was llenado with a sound of thunder, the suelo rocked under his feet, and a terrible looking beast apareció in frente of him.

"Miserable man!" cried the Beast, "what have you done? All the best in the castillo was ofrecido to you. Why have you broken my rose arbusto that is dearer to me than anything in the world? Now for this you must surely morir."

The merchant was terrified.

"Oh, dear, good Beast please do not kill me!" he cried. "I meant no harm. Please let me go, and I will never molestar you again."

"No, no," answered the Beast. "You shall not escapar so easily. You have broken my rose-arbusto and you must sufrir for it."

C.2.06

Still the merchant rogó and pleaded to be perdonado and at last the Beast had pity on him. "If I perdono your life," he said, "what will you give me in retorno for it?"

"Alas," said the merchant, "what can I give you? I have lost all my fortune and I am now a pobre man. I have nothing left in the world but my three hijas."

"Give me one of your hijas for an esposa and I will be satisfecho," said the Beast.

The merchant was horrorizado at the thought of such a thing. He wanted to refuse, but he was asustado that if he did so, the Beast would tear him to pieces.

"You can have three meses in which to think it over," said the Beast. "But you must promise me that at the end of that time you will regresar here and either traer me one of your hijas or come preparado to morir."

The merchant was obligado to promise this; he could not ayudar himself. As soon as he had promised the Beast desapareció and the man was free to go, and so he went quickly.

C.2.07

He rode on toward his home but his corazón was pesado inside his pecho. He did not see how he could posiblemente give one of his hijas to be the novia of an espantoso beast, and yet he did not want to morir.

His hijas met him with joy, and the two older hermanas were delighted when they saw the beautiful regalos he had traído them. Only Beauty notó his sad and downcast looks.

"Dear father," said she, "why are you preocupado? Has something bad happened to you?"

At first her father would not tell her, but she urged and rogó him to tell her until finally he could not keep silencio any longer. He told his hijas all about the castillo and what happened there, and of the Beast, and of how unless one of them would consentir to marry the Beast he would have to lose his life.

When the older hijas heard this they nearly fainted. Even to save their father's life they could not consentir to marry such a criatura.

"Dear father," said Beauty, "you shall not morir. I will be the Beast's novia."

"Yes, yes," cried her hermanas. "That is only right. If Beauty had not asked for the rose this problema would not have happened."

C.2.08

At first the merchant would not agree to this. Beauty was the dearest to him of all his hijas. He had hoped that if any of them was to marry the Beast it might be one of the older hermanas. But they would not escuchar of this and when, at the end of three meses, the merchant set out to regresar to the castillo he took Beauty with him.

They rode along and rode along and after a while they came to the forest, and it did not take the merchant long to find the castillo. He knocked on the door, and it opened as before, and he and Beauty went in through one room after another, and everything was so magnífico that she had to admirar it. At last, they came to the dining room, and here a delicioso banquete was set out for them.

They sat down and ate while soft música sounded around them.

Beauty began to think the master of all this could not be such a terrible criatura after all.

C.2.09

But as soon as they finished their cena the Beast apareció in frente of them, and when Beauty saw him she began to agitar and tremble, for he was even more dreadful looking than her father had said.

"Do not be temerosa of me, Beauty," he said in a suave voice. "I will do you no harm. Your father has traído you here, and it is true that you must permanecer here, but you do not have to marry me unless you are sure you are dispuesto to."

"I do not want to marry you, Beast, and you must know that," said Beauty. "But I am asustado that if I do not marry you, you will harm my father."

"No, Beauty, I will not harm him. He may go in peace, and perhaps after you have been here a while you may learn to like me enough to marry me."

Beauty did not creer this, but the Beast habló so suavemente that she no longer feared him, and when the time came for her father to go she said goodbye to him and did not sadden him by crying.

C.2.10

After that Beauty lived there in the Beast's castillo and was contenta. Every day she went out into the jardines, and the Beast came and played with her for a while, and she creció very fond of him. Every day before he left her he said, "Beauty, are you dispuesto to marry me?"

But Beauty always answered,

"No, dear Beast, I do not desear to marry you."

Then the Beast would suspirar fuertemente and go away.

One day Beauty was sitting in frente of a large espejo in her room, and she was sad because she had not seen her father for so long.

"I deseo," said she, "that I could see what my dear father is doing at this very moment."

As she said this, she raised her eyes to the espejo. She was very sorprendido to see in the espejo a reflexión of a room completely diferente to the one she was in. It was a room in her own home that she saw reflejada there. She saw in it the imágenes of her father and hermanas. She could see them sonreir and move, and she could tell exactly what they were doing. She found she could watch them in the espejo for as long as she pleased and whenever she pleased.

C.2.11

After this Beauty often came to sit in frente of the espejo, and she only had to desear it and she could see her home, and all that was going on there.

But one day, when she sat down in frente of the espejo, she saw that her father was enfermo. He was lying on his bed so pálido and weak that Beauty was terrified. She jumped up and ran out into the jardín calling for the Beast.

At once he apareció in frente of her. "What is it?" asked the Beast anxiously. "What has frightened you, Beauty?"

"Alas," she cried, "my father is enfermo. Oh dear kind Beast, please let me go to him, and I will love you for ever after."

The Beast looked very grave.

"Very well, Beauty," he said, "I will let you go, for I can refuse you nothing. But promise me you will regresar at the end of a semana, for if you do not some great desgracia will happen to me."

C.2.12

Beauty was very dispuesto to promise this. The Beast then gave her an anillo with a large rubí. "When you go to bed esta noche," he said, "turn the rubí in toward the palma of your hand and desea you were in your father's house, and in the morning, you will find you are there. When you are ready to regresar do the same thing, and you will find yourself back in the castillo again.

But do not forget, that by the end of a semana, to an hour, you must regresar or you will traer sufrimiento upon me."

Beauty did as the Beast told her. That noche when she lay down, she turned the rubí of the anillo in toward the palma of her hand and deseó she was in her father's house. She was very happy, when she woke up the next morning, and found herself in her own bed at home. She got up and ran to her father's room, and the merchant was so delighted to see her that, from that hour, he began to get better, and in a few days he was as well as ever again.

C.2.13

Beauty's hermanas asked her a lot of questions about the castillo where she lived, and when they heard how fine it was, and how happy she was there, they were llenado with envidia.

"Beauty always gets the best of everything," they said to each other. "She is younger than either of nosotros, but look how finely she lives; much better than we do."

Then they planificaron together as to how they could keep Beauty from going back to the castillo at the end of the semana.

"If we can only make her romper her promise to the Beast," they said, "he might be so angry with her that he will send her away and take one of nosotros to live at his castillo instead."

The day before Beauty was due to regresar to the Beast, they put some sleeping powder in the cáliz that she drank from.

As soon as Beauty had swallowed the powder she became very sleepy. Her párpados weighed like lead, and soon she fell into a profundo duermevela, and she did not wake up for two days and noches.

C.2.14

At the end of that time Beauty had a dream, and in her dream she walked in the castillo jardines. She came to the rose-arbusto beside the fuente, and there lay the pobre Beast estirado out on the suelo, and he was almost dead. He opened his eyes and looked at her sadly.

"Ah, Beauty, Beauty," he said, "why did you romper your promise to regresar at the end of a semana? See what sufrimiento you have traído on me."

Beauty woke up, sobbing amargamente.

"Alas, alas!" she cried. "I must go at once. I feel some harm has come to the Beast, and that it is my culpa, though how, I do not know." She did not realise she had been asleep for two days and noches.

She turned the rubí anillo with the rubí toward the palma of her hand, and deseó herself back in the castillo and then lay down and went to sleep.

C.2.15

When she woke up she was in the castillo again, and it was early morning. She ran out into the jardín, and straight to the rose-arbusto. There, as in her dream, she saw the Beast estirado out on the suelo, and he seemed to be without life or breath. Beauty threw herself down on the suelo and took his head in her lap, and her tears ran down and fell upon him, and it seemed to her she did not love even her father as dearly as she loved the Beast.

"Oh, Beast - dear, dear Beast," she cried, "can you escuchar me? Are you realmente dead?"

Then the Beast opened his eyes and looked at her.

"Ah, Beauty," he said, "I thought you had deserted me. Do you still not love me enough to marry me?"

"Oh, I do! I do love you enough, and gladly I will be your novia," cried Beauty.

No sooner had she said this than the rough furry hide of the Beast fell aparte, and a guapo young príncipe, dressed in white satin and silver stood in frente of her. Beauty looked at him in wonder.

C.2.16

"Yes, you shall indeed be my own dear novia," cried the Príncipe, "for you and you alone have broken the hechizo that held me."

Then the Príncipe, a Beast no longer, told Beauty that a malvada hada had cambiado him into the forma of a Beast, and not until a fair young doncella could love him enough to be his novia would the hechizo be broken.

But Beauty had loved him for his kindness and goodness in spite of his ugly forma, and now never again could the malvada hada have any poder over him.

And now all through the castillo the sound of life and voices was heard, and of people running to and fro. For the same hechizo that had cambiado the Príncipe to a Beast had made all his people invisible, and now, they too were freed from the hechizo.

C.2.17

Now Beauty was very happy. If she had loved the Beast, she loved the guapo young Príncipe a thousand times more. A gran wedding banquete was preparado, and her father and hermanas were sent for. Her father was given the place of honor, but it was quite diferente with her hermanas; because of their hard corazones they were cambiado into two estatuas and they stood one on either side of the doorway.

But Beauty was too amable to be angry with them. After she was married she often used to go and stand beside the estatuas and talk to them, and her tears fell upon them so that after a while their hard corazones crecieron soft and the stone derretió back to flesh again. Then they were all very happy together. The two hermanas married two nobles of the corte.

As for Beauty and the Príncipe, nothing could igual their love for each other, and they lived together happy forever after, and no further harm ever came to them.

Beauty and the Beast

C.3.01

There was once a comerciante who had three hijas. The two older ones were pretty enough, but the third was a beauty, and no mistake. Her eyes were as azul as the cielo, her hair was as black as ebony, and her cheeks were like roses. The comerciante loved his two older hijas dearly, but he loved Beauty even more dearly.

Things went along pleasantly for a long time, and the comerciante was rich and prosperous, but then things began to go wrong for him. One after another, his ships were perdidos at sea, and a large part of his fortune was perdido with them.

So, one day, the comerciante called his hijas to him and said, "My children, I need to go on a long journey. I am no longer a rich man, but I deseo to traer home a gift for each one of you, so tell me what you would like to have."

The two older hijas began to think of all the things they wanted, and each was afraid the other would get something finer than she did.

C.3.02

At last the eldest habló, "Dear father," said she, "I deseo you would traer me a velvet robe embroidered with gold, and shoes to match, and a fan to wave in my hand."

"And I," said the second, "would like a necklace of perlas, and perlas for my hair, and a fine bracelet."

The comerciante was preocupado that his hijas should ask for such expensive things, but he did not like to refuse them.

"And you, Beauty," he said, turning to his youngest hija, "what would you like?"

"Dear father," she said, "you have given me so much that I have nothing left to desear for; but if you traes me anything at all let it be a rose."

When her older hermanas heard this they were very angry. They thought that Beauty had asked only for a rose so that she would shame them in frente of their father, and make him think she was less selfish than they were. But Beauty had had no such thought as that.

The comerciante smiled at his youngest hija and kissed her three times, but he only kissed his older hijas once. Then he got on his horse and rode away.

C.3.03

He travelled on for several days, and at last he reached the city he was going to. Here he discovered that he had perdido even more of his fortune than he had thought. He was now a pobre man.

Still, he managed to buy the gifts his two older hijas had asked for, and then with a sad corazón he set out for home.

He had not travelled far, however, when he was overtaken by a storm and got perdido in a deep forest. He rode this way and that, trying to find the way out, and then suddenly he came to an open place, and there he saw a magnífico castillo in frente of him.

The comerciante was amazed. He had never heard of such a castillo in that forest. He rode up to the door and knocked, hoping to find shelter for the noche.

As soon as he knocked on the great door, it swung open in frente of him. He went in and looked around, no one was there; everything was silencioso.

C.3.04

He went on into one room after another. Everything was very magnífico and well arranged, but there was not a soul to be seen. At last he came to a room where a cena was set out. The plates were all of gold, and the meats and fruits were of the rarest and most deliciosas kinds.

The comerciante was so hungry that he sat down at the table, and at once the food was served to him by invisible hands, while soft música sounded from a hidden room beyond.

He ate well and then got up and went to look for a place to sleep. He soon found a place. A bed had been made ready in a large room, and he undressed there, and, lying down, he slept until morning without being disturbed.

When he woke up, he found his own dirty clothes had been taken away. In their place a bonito suit had been extendido out, of the richest kind. There was also a bag lleno with gold pieces. Wondering still more, the comerciante got up and dressed and went out into the jardines to look around.

C.3.05

Here everything was more beautiful than any jardín he had ever seen before. There were winding paths and fountains, and fruit trees and flowering plants.

Beside one of the fountains was a rose arbusto covered with roses. The sight of the roses reminded the comerciante of Beauty's deseo, and he thought it would do no harm to romper off one to take to her. He chose the largest and finest rose. But, the moment he plucked it, the air was llenado with a sound of thunder, the suelo rocked under his feet, and a terrible looking beast appeared in frente of him.

"Miserable man!" cried the Beast, "what have you done? All the best in the castillo was offered to you. Why have you broken my rose arbusto that is dearer to me than anything in the world? Now for this you must surely morir."

The comerciante was terrified.

Beauty and the Beast

"Oh, dear, good Beast please do not kill me!" he cried. "I meant no harm. Please let me go, and I will never molestar you again."

"No, no," answered the Beast. "You shall not escape so easily. You have broken my rose-arbusto and you must sufrir for it."

C.3.06

Still the comerciante rogó and pleaded to be spared and at last the Beast had pity on him. "If I spare your life," he said, "what will you give me in retorno for it?"

"Alas," said the comerciante, "what can I give you? I have perdido all my fortune and I am now a pobre man. I have nothing left in the world but my three hijas."

"Give me one of your hijas for an esposa and I will be satisfecho," said the Beast.

The comerciante was horrified at the thought of such a thing. He wanted to refuse, but he was asustado that if he did so, the Beast would tear him to pieces.

"You can have three months in which to think it over," said the Beast. "But you must promise me that at the end of that time you will regresar here and either traer me one of your hijas or come preparado to die."

The comerciante was obliged to promise this; he could not ayudar himself. As soon as he had promised the Beast disappeared and the man was free to go, and so he went quickly.

C.3.07

He rode on toward his home but his corazón was heavy inside his chest. He did not see how he could possibly give one of his hijas to be the novia of a hideous beast, and yet he did not want to die.

His hijas met him with joy, and the two older hermanas were delighted when they saw the beautiful gifts he had traído them. Only Beauty noticed his sad and downcast looks.

"Dear father," said she, "why are you preocupado? Has something bad happened to you?"

At first her father would not tell her, but she urged and rogó him to tell her until finally he could not keep silencio any longer. He told his hijas all about the castillo and what happened there, and of the Beast, and of how unless one of them would consent to marry the Beast he would have to lose his life.

When the older hijas heard this they nearly fainted. Even to save their father's life they could not consent to marry such a criatura.

"Dear father," said Beauty, "you shall not die. I will be the Beast's novia."

"Yes, yes," cried her hermanas. "That is only right. If Beauty had not asked for the rose this problema would not have happened."

C.3.08

At first the comerciante would not agree to this. Beauty was the dearest to him of all his hijas. He had hoped that if any of them was to marry the Beast it might be one of the older hermanas. But they would not escuchar of this and when, at the end of three months, the comerciante set out to regresar to the castillo he took Beauty with him.

Beauty and the Beast

They rode along and rode along and after a while they came to the forest, and it did not take the comerciante long to find the castillo. He knocked on the door, and it opened as before, and he and Beauty went in through one room after another, and everything was so magnífico that she had to admire it. At last, they came to the dining room, and here a delicioso banquete was set out for them.

They sat down and ate while soft música sounded around them. Beauty began to think the master of all this could not be such a terrible criatura after all.

C.3.09

But as soon as they finished their cena the Beast appeared in frente of them, and when Beauty saw him she began to shake and tremble, for he was even more dreadful looking than her father had said.

"Do not be afraid of me, Beauty," he said in a gentle voice. "I will do you no harm. Your father has traído you here, and it is true that you must stay here, but you do not have to marry me unless you are sure you are dispuesto to."

"I do not want to marry you, Beast, and you must know that," said Beauty. "But I am asustada that if I do not marry you, you will harm my father."

"No, Beauty, I will not harm him. He may go in peace, and perhaps after you have been here a while you may learn to like me enough to marry me."

Beauty did not creer this, but the Beast habló so gently that she no longer feared him, and when the time came for her father to go she said goodbye to him and did not sadden him by weeping.

C.3.10

After that Beauty lived there in the Beast's castillo and was content. Every day she went out into the jardines, and the Beast came and played with her for a while, and she grew very fond of him. Every day before he left her he said, "Beauty, are you dispuesto to marry me?"

But Beauty always answered,

"No, dear Beast, I do not desear to marry you."

Then the Beast would sigh heavily and go away.

One day Beauty was sitting in frente of a large espejo in her room, and she was sad because she had not seen her father for so long.

"I deseo," said she, "that I could see what my dear father is doing at this very moment."

As she said this, she raised her eyes to the espejo. She was very sorprendido to see in the espejo a reflection of a room completely diferente to the one she was in. It was a room in her own home that she saw reflected there. She saw in it the images of her father and hermanas. She could see them smile and move, and she could tell exactly what they were doing. She found she could watch them in the espejo for as long as she pleased and whenever she pleased.

C.3.11

After this Beauty often came to sit in frente of the espejo, and she only had to desear it and she could see her home, and all that was going on there.

But one day, when she sat down in frente of the espejo, she saw that her father was ill. He was lying on his bed so pálido and weak that Beauty was terrified. She jumped up and ran out into the jardín calling for the Beast.

Beauty and the Beast

At once he appeared in frente of her. "What is it?" asked the Beast anxiously. "What has frightened you, Beauty?"

"Alas," she cried, "my father is ill. Oh dear kind Beast, please let me go to him, and I will love you for ever after."

The Beast looked very serious.

"Very well, Beauty," he said, "I will let you go, for I can refuse you nothing. But promise me you will regresar at the end of a semana, for if you do not some great misfortune will happen to me."

C.3.12

Beauty was very dispuesto to promise this. The Beast then gave her an anillo with a large rubí. "When you go to bed esta noche," he said, "turn the rubí in toward the palma of your hand and desea you were in your father's house, and in the morning, you will find you are there. When you are ready to regresar do the same thing, and you will find yourself back in the castillo again.

But do not forget, that by the end of a semana, to an hour, you must regresar or you will traer sufrimiento upon me."

Beauty did as the Beast told her. That noche when she lay down, she turned the rubí of the anillo in toward the palma of her hand and deseó she was in her father's house. She was very happy, when she woke up the next morning, and found herself in her own bed at home. She got up and ran to her father's room, and the comerciante was so delighted to see her that, from that hour, he began to get better, and in a few days he was as well as ever again.

C.3.13

Beauty's hermanas asked her a lot of questions about the castillo where she lived, and when they heard how fine it was, and how happy she was there, they were llenado with envy.

"Beauty always gets the best of everything," they said to each other. "She is younger than either of nosotros, but look how finely she lives; much better than we do."

Then they planned together as to how they could keep Beauty from going back to the castillo at the end of the semana.

"If we can only make her romper her promise to the Beast," they said, "he might be so angry with her that he will send her away and take one of nosotros to live at his castillo instead."

The day before Beauty was due to regresar to the Beast, they put some sleeping powder in the goblet that she drank from.

As soon as Beauty had swallowed the powder she became very sleepy. Her eyelids weighed like lead, and soon she fell into a deep slumber, and she did not wake up for two days and noches.

C.3.14

At the end of that time Beauty had a dream, and in her dream she walked in the castillo jardines. She came to the rose-arbusto beside the fountain, and there lay the pobre Beast estirado out on the suelo, and he was almost dead. He opened his eyes and looked at her sadly.

"Ah, Beauty, Beauty," he said, "why did you romper your promise to regresar at the end of a semana? See what sufrimiento you have traído on me."

Beauty woke up, sobbing bitterly.

"Alas, alas!" she cried. "I must go at once. I feel some harm has come to the Beast, and that it is my fault, though how, I do not know." She did not realise she had been asleep for two days and noches.

She turned the rubí anillo with the rubí toward the palma of her hand, and deseó herself back in the castillo and then lay down and went to sleep.

C.3.15

When she woke up she was in the castillo again, and it was early morning. She ran out into the jardín, and straight to the rose-arbusto. There, as in her dream, she saw the Beast estirado out on the suelo, and he seemed to be without life or breath. Beauty threw herself down on the suelo and took his head in her lap, and her tears ran down and fell upon him, and it seemed to her she did not love even her father as dearly as she loved the Beast.

"Oh, Beast - dear, dear Beast," she cried, "can you escuchar me? Are you really dead?"

Then the Beast opened his eyes and looked at her.

"Ah, Beauty," he said, "I thought you had deserted me. Do you still not love me enough to marry me?"

"Oh, I do! I do love you enough, and gladly I will be your novia," cried Beauty.

No sooner had she said this than the rough furry hide of the Beast fell apart, and a guapo young príncipe, dressed in white satin and silver stood in frente of her. Beauty looked at him in wonder.

C.3.16

"Yes, you shall indeed be my own dear novia," cried the Príncipe, "for you and you alone have broken the hechizo that held me."

Then the Príncipe, a Beast no longer, told Beauty that a wicked hada had cambiado him into the shape of a Beast, and not until a fair young maiden could love him enough to be his novia would the hechizo be broken.

But Beauty had loved him for his kindness and goodness in spite of his ugly form, and now never again could the wicked hada have any power over him.

And now all through the castillo the sound of life and voices was heard, and of people running to and fro. For the same hechizo that had cambiado the Príncipe to a Beast had made all his people invisible, and now, they too were freed from the hechizo.

C.3.17

Now Beauty was very happy. If she had loved the Beast, she loved the guapo young Príncipe a thousand times more. A grand wedding banquete was preparado, and her father and hermanas were sent for. Her father was given the place of honour, but it was quite diferente with her hermanas; because of their hard corazones they were cambiado into two estatuas and they stood one on either side of the doorway.

But Beauty was too gentle to be angry with them. After she was married she often used to go and stand beside the estatuas and talk to them, and her tears fell upon them so that after a while their hard corazones grew soft and the stone derretió back to flesh again. Then they were all very happy together. The two hermanas married two noblemen of the court.

As for Beauty and the Príncipe, nothing could equal their love for each other, and they lived together happy forever after, and no further harm ever came to them.

Beauty and the Beast

C.4.01

There was once a merchant who had three daughters. The two older ones were pretty enough, but the third was a beauty, and no mistake. Her eyes were as blue as the sky, her hair was as black as ebony, and her cheeks were like roses. The merchant loved his two older daughters dearly, but he loved Beauty even more dearly.

Things went along pleasantly for a long time, and the merchant was rich and prosperous, but then things began to go wrong for him. One after another, his ships were lost at sea, and a large part of his fortune was lost with them.

So, one day, the merchant called his daughters to him and said, "My children, I need to go on a long journey. I am no longer a rich man, but I wish to bring home a gift for each one of you, so tell me what you would like to have."

The two older daughters began to think of all the things they wanted, and each was afraid the other would get something finer than she did.

C.4.02

At last the eldest spoke, "Dear father," said she, "I wish you would bring me a velvet robe embroidered with gold, and shoes to match, and a fan to wave in my hand."

"And I," said the second, "would like a necklace of pearls, and pearls for my hair, and a fine bracelet."

The merchant was troubled that his daughters should ask for such expensive things, but he did not like to refuse them.

"And you, Beauty," he said, turning to his youngest daughter, "what would you like?"

"Dear father," she said, "you have given me so much that I have nothing left to wish for; but if you bring me anything at all let it be a rose."

When her older sisters heard this they were very angry. They thought that Beauty had asked only for a rose so that she would shame them in front of their father, and make him think she was less selfish than they were. But Beauty had had no such thought as that.

The merchant smiled at his youngest daughter and kissed her three times, but he only kissed his older daughters once. Then he got on his horse and rode away.

C.4.03

He travelled on for several days, and at last he reached the city he was going to. Here he discovered that he had lost even more of his fortune than he had thought. He was now a poor man.

Still, he managed to buy the gifts his two older daughters had asked for, and then with a sad heart he set out for home.

He had not travelled far, however, when he was overtaken by a storm and got lost in a deep forest. He rode this way and that, trying to find the way out, and then suddenly he came to an open place, and there he saw a magnificent castle in front of him.

The merchant was amazed. He had never heard of such a castle in that forest. He rode up to the door and knocked, hoping to find shelter for the night.

As soon as he knocked on the great door, it swung open in front of him. He went in and looked around, no one was there; everything was silent.

C.4.04

He went on into one room after another. Everything was very magnificent and well arranged, but there was not a soul to be seen. At last he came to a room where a supper was set out. The plates were all of gold, and the meats and fruits were of the rarest and most delicious kinds.

The merchant was so hungry that he sat down at the table, and at once the food was served to him by invisible hands, while soft music sounded from a hidden room beyond.

He ate well and then got up and went to look for a place to sleep. He soon found a place. A bed had been made ready in a large room, and he undressed there, and, lying down, he slept until morning without being disturbed.

When he woke up, he found his own dirty clothes had been taken away. In their place a handsome suit had been laid out, of the richest kind. There was also a bag filled with gold pieces. Wondering still more, the merchant got up and dressed and went out into the gardens to look around.

C.4.05

Here everything was more beautiful than any garden he had ever seen before. There were winding paths and fountains, and fruit trees and flowering plants.

Beside one of the fountains was a rose bush covered with roses. The sight of the roses reminded the merchant of Beauty's wish, and he thought it would do no harm to break off one to take to her. He chose the largest and finest rose. But, the moment he plucked it, the air was filled with a sound of thunder, the ground rocked under his feet, and a terrible looking beast appeared in front of him.

"Miserable man!" cried the Beast, "what have you done? All the best in the castle was offered to you. Why have you broken my rose bush that is dearer to me than anything in the world? Now for this you must surely die."

The merchant was terrified.

"Oh, dear, good Beast please do not kill me!" he cried. "I meant no harm. Please let me go, and I will never trouble you again."

"No, no," answered the Beast. "You shall not escape so easily. You have broken my rose-bush and you must suffer for it."

C.4.06

Still the merchant begged and pleaded to be spared and at last the Beast had pity on him. "If I spare your life," he said, "what will you give me in return for it?"

"Alas," said the merchant, "what can I give you? I have lost all my fortune and I am now a poor man. I have nothing left in the world but my three daughters."

"Give me one of your daughters for a wife and I will be satisfied," said the Beast.

The merchant was horrified at the thought of such a thing. He wanted to refuse, but he was scared that if he did so, the Beast would tear him to pieces.

"You can have three months in which to think it over," said the Beast. "But you must promise me that at the end of that time you will return here and either bring me one of your daughters or come prepared to die."

The merchant was obliged to promise this; he could not help himself. As soon as he had promised the Beast disappeared and the man was free to go, and so he went quickly.

C.4.07

He rode on toward his home but his heart was heavy inside his chest. He did not see how he could possibly give one of his daughters to be the bride of a hideous beast, and yet he did not want to die.

His daughters met him with joy, and the two older sisters were delighted when they saw the beautiful gifts he had brought them. Only Beauty noticed his sad and downcast looks.

"Dear father," said she, "why are you troubled? Has something bad happened to you?"

At first her father would not tell her, but she urged and begged him to tell her until finally he could not keep silent any longer. He told his daughters all about the castle and what happened there, and of the Beast, and of how unless one of them would consent to marry the Beast he would have to lose his life.

When the older daughters heard this they nearly fainted. Even to save their father's life they could not consent to marry such a creature.

"Dear father," said Beauty, "you shall not die. I will be the Beast's bride."

"Yes, yes," cried her sisters. "That is only right. If Beauty had not asked for the rose this trouble would not have happened."

C.4.08

At first the merchant would not agree to this. Beauty was the dearest to him of all his daughters. He had hoped that if any of them was to marry the Beast it might be one of the older sisters. But they would not hear of this and when, at the end of three months, the merchant set out to return to the castle he took Beauty with him.

They rode along and rode along and after a while they came to the forest, and it did not take the merchant long to find the castle. He knocked on the door, and it opened as before, and he and Beauty went in through one room after another, and everything was so magnificent that she had to admire it. At last, they came to the dining room, and here a delicious feast was set out for them.

They sat down and ate while soft music sounded around them. Beauty began to think the master of all this could not be such a terrible creature after all.

C.4.09

But as soon as they finished their supper the Beast appeared in front of them, and when Beauty saw him she began to shake and tremble, for he was even more dreadful looking than her father had said.

"Do not be afraid of me, Beauty," he said in a gentle voice. "I will do you no harm. Your father has brought you here, and it is true that you must stay here, but you do not have to marry me unless you are sure you are willing to."

"I do not want to marry you, Beast, and you must know that," said Beauty. "But I am scared that if I do not marry you, you will harm my father."

"No, Beauty, I will not harm him. He may go in peace, and perhaps after you have been here a while you may learn to like me enough to marry me."

Beauty did not believe this, but the Beast spoke so gently that she no longer feared him, and when the time came for her father to go she said goodbye to him and did not sadden him by weeping.

C.4.10

After that Beauty lived there in the Beast's castle and was content. Every day she went out into the gardens, and the Beast came and played with her for a while, and she grew very fond of him. Every day before he left her he said, "Beauty, are you willing to marry me?"

But Beauty always answered,

"No, dear Beast, I do not wish to marry you."

Then the Beast would sigh heavily and go away.

One day Beauty was sitting in front of a large mirror in her room, and she was sad because she had not seen her father for so long.

"I wish," said she, "that I could see what my dear father is doing at this very moment."

As she said this, she raised her eyes to the mirror. She was very surprised to see in the mirror a reflection of a room completely different to the one she was in. It was a room in her own home that she saw reflected there. She saw in it the images of her father and sisters. She could see them smile and move, and she could tell exactly what they were doing. She found she could watch them in the mirror for as long as she pleased and whenever she pleased.

C.4.11

After this Beauty often came to sit in front of the mirror, and she only had to wish it and she could see her home, and all that was going on there.

But one day, when she sat down in front of the mirror, she saw that her father was ill. He was lying on his bed so pale and weak that Beauty was terrified. She jumped up and ran out into the garden calling for the Beast.

At once he appeared in front of her. "What is it?" asked the Beast anxiously. "What has frightened you, Beauty?"

"Alas," she cried, "my father is ill. Oh dear kind Beast, please let me go to him, and I will love you for ever after."

The Beast looked very serious.

"Very well, Beauty," he said, "I will let you go, for I can refuse you nothing. But promise me you will return at the end of a week, for if you do not some great misfortune will happen to me."

C.4.12

Beauty was very willing to promise this. The Beast then gave her a ring with a large ruby. "When you go to bed tonight," he said, "turn the ruby in toward the palm of your hand and wish you were in your father's house, and in the morning, you will find you are there. When you are ready to return do the same thing, and you will find yourself back in the castle again.

But do not forget, that by the end of a week, to an hour, you must return or you will bring suffering upon me."

Beauty did as the Beast told her. That night when she lay down, she turned the ruby of the ring in toward the palm of her hand and wished she was in her father's house. She was very happy, when she woke up the next morning, and found herself in her own bed at home. She got up and ran to her father's room, and the merchant was so delighted to see her that, from that hour, he began to get better, and in a few days he was as well as ever again.

C.4.13

Beauty's sisters asked her a lot of questions about the castle where she lived, and when they heard how fine it was, and how happy she was there, they were filled with envy.

"Beauty always gets the best of everything," they said to each other. "She is younger than either of us, but look how finely she lives; much better than we do."

Then they planned together as to how they could keep Beauty from going back to the castle at the end of the week.

"If we can only make her break her promise to the Beast," they said, "he might be so angry with her that he will send her away and take one of us to live at his castle instead."

The day before Beauty was due to regresar to the Beast, they put some sleeping powder in the goblet that she drank from.

As soon as Beauty had swallowed the powder she became very sleepy. Her eyelids weighed like lead, and soon she fell into a deep slumber, and she did not wake up for two days and nights.

C.4.14

At the end of that time Beauty had a dream, and in her dream she walked in the castle gardens. She came to the rose-bush beside the fountain, and there lay the poor Beast stretched out on the ground, and he was almost dead. He opened his eyes and looked at her sadly.

"Ah, Beauty, Beauty," he said, "why did you break your promise to return at the end of a week? See what suffering you have brought on me."

Beauty woke up, sobbing bitterly.

"Alas, alas!" she cried. "I must go at once. I feel some harm has come to the Beast, and that it is my fault, though how, I do not sabe." She did not realise she had been asleep for two days and nights.

She turned the ruby ring with the ruby toward the palm of her hand, and wished herself back in the castle and then lay down and went to sleep.

C.4.15

When she woke up she was in the castle again, and it was early morning. She ran out into the garden, and straight to the rose-bush. There, as in her dream, she saw the Beast stretched out on the ground, and he seemed to be without life or breath. Beauty threw herself down on the ground and took his head in her lap, and her tears ran down and fell upon him, and it seemed to her she did not love even her father as dearly as she loved the Beast.

"Oh, Beast - dear, dear Beast," she cried, "can you hear me? Are you really dead?"

Then the Beast opened his eyes and looked at her.

"Ah, Beauty," he said, "I thought you had deserted me. Do you still not love me enough to marry me?"

"Oh, I do! I do love you enough, and gladly I will be your bride," cried Beauty.

No sooner had she said this than the rough furry hide of the Beast fell apart, and a handsome young prince, dressed in white satin and silver stood in front of her. Beauty looked at him in wonder.

C.4.16

"Yes, you shall indeed be my own dear bride," cried the Prince, "for you and you alone have broken the spell that held me."

Then the Prince, a Beast no longer, told Beauty that a wicked fairy had changed him into the shape of a Beast, and not until a fair young maiden could love him enough to be his bride would the spell be broken.

But Beauty had loved him for his kindness and goodness in spite of his ugly form, and now never again could the wicked fairy have any power over him.

And now all through the castle the sound of life and voices was heard, and of people running to and fro. For the same spell that had changed the Prince to a Beast had made all his people invisible, and now, they too were freed from the spell.

C.4.17

Now Beauty was very happy. If she had loved the Beast, she loved the handsome young Prince a thousand times more. A grand wedding feast was prepared, and her father and sisters were sent for. Her father was given the place of honour, but it was quite different with her sisters; because of their hard hearts they were changed into two statues and they stood one on either side of the doorway.

But Beauty was too gentle to be angry with them. After she was married she often used to go and stand beside the statues and talk to them, and her tears fell upon them so that after a while their hard hearts grew soft and the stone melted back to flesh again. Then they were all very happy together. The two sisters married two noblemen of the court.

Beauty and the Beast

As for Beauty and the Prince, nothing could equal their love for each other, and they lived together happy forever after, and no further harm ever came to them.

D
Notas finales

Beauty and the Beast sólo tiene cuatro niveles. Te sugiero que leas el nivel C.4 dos o tres veces para que te familiarices con el vocabulario, pero no lo estudies en detalle. Cuando puedas leer y comprender el nivel C.4 razonablemente bien, continúa con el libro 5, *Jack and the Bean Stalk*.

La siguiente sección es Un poco de gramática, pero este apartado no es imprescindible. Si no te gusta estudiar gramática, ignora la sección E y continúa con el libro 5.

E
Un poco de gramática – Verbos compuestos

E.1 Verbos Compuestos – Introducción

El inglés tiene una gran cantidad de construcciones verbales; «*phrasal verbs*» / «verbos compuestos» que normalmente se traducirían con una sola palabra en castellano.

Un verbo compuesto en inglés consiste en un verbo seguido de otra palabra o palabras para formar una frase.

Por lo general, el verbo es común y corto, que puede tener múltiples significados incluso cuando se usa sólo como un verbo simple.

Del mismo modo, las palabras que siguen a estos verbos también suelen ser muy cortas y tienen múltiples significados como palabras únicas.

La frase formada por un verbo compuesto suele tener un significado nuevo que es independiente de las palabras de la frase.

Algunos ejemplos serían:

to go up / to come up – **ascender**;

to go down / to come down – descender;

to go in / to come in – entrar;

to go out / to come out – salir.

Los ejemplos anteriores son bastante claros. Sin embargo, en la mayoría de los casos, la traducción de los verbos compuestos del inglés al castellano no es muy obvia:

Victoria sat down – Victoria se sentó;

Victoria sat up – Victoria se enderezó (mientras estaba sentada);

Victoria stood up – Victoria se puso de pie;

Victoria got up – Victoria se puso de pie / Victoria se levantó;

Victoria went out with David – Victoria tenía una cita con David;

Victoria went down with a cold – Victoria cayó con un resfriado;

Victoria was very down with her friend – Victoria estaba muy deprimida con su amiga.

El mayor problema de un hablante de castellano para aprender los verbos compuestos es, en primer lugar, simplemente reconocerlos.

De los aproximadamente cuatrocientos verbos compuestos más comunes en inglés, estas frases incluían muchos verbos diferentes.

Sin embargo, estos verbos compuestos incluían sólo treinta y tres segundas o terceras palabras. Estas se enumeran en la tabla E.1 a continuación:

Tabla E.1				
about	around	down	off	together
across	at	for	on	toward
after	away	forward	out	up
against	back	from	over	with
ahead	behind	in	past	without
along	beyond	into	through	
apart	by	of	to	

Esta no es una lista exhaustiva, pero incluye casi todos los verbos compuestos que probablemente encontrarás.

Entonces, el primer truco para detectar los verbos compuestos es fijarse en las palabras de la tabla E.1.

Si ves una de estas palabras y no parece tener su significado normal o parece confusa, significa que es probable que forme parte de un verbo compuesto.

De modo que, si ves una de las palabras de la tabla E.1 anterior, entonces debes buscar el verbo que esté delante de esta palabra. Generalmente es un verbo común corto.

Luego, puedes buscar el significado del verbo más la preposición en Internet o en un diccionario de verbos compuestos. (Recomiendo encarecidamente que cualquier estudiante de inglés compre un buen diccionario de verbos compuestos en inglés).

Un segundo problema para identificarlos verbos compuestos es recordar que muchos verbos comunes del inglés tienen tiempos irregulares.

El caso más obvio son los verbos compuestos que usan «*to go*», que comúnmente se encuentran usando la forma de tiempo pasado «*went*».

Victoria went away – Victoria se fue / Victoria se alejó.

Esto también puede resultar confuso con el tiempo pasado de muchos otros verbos como «*get / got*», «*be / was / were*», «*have / has / had*», etc.

Un tercer problema con los verbos compuestos es que pueden estar conformados por tres palabras.

look up to – admirar a alguien;

look forward to – anticipar (algo bueno);

come up with – proponer (una buena idea);

feel up to (something) – tener la energía o la confianza (para hacer algo); etc.

Sin embargo, el mayor problema al reconocer los verbos compuestos es que estos pueden aparecer divididos en una oración.

Entonces, en la siguiente oración «*went… up*» es una forma del verbo compuesto «*to go up*» que significa «subir»:

Victoria went slowly up the stairs – Victoria subió lentamente las escaleras.

Esto también aplica para la siguiente oración, aunque hay ocho palabras y tres signos de puntuación entre «*went*» y «*up*».

Victoria went slowly, carefully, and not without a little fear, up the stairs – Victoria subió lentamente, con cuidado, y no sin un poco de miedo, las escaleras.

Los siguientes son todos ejemplos de verbos compuestos que se encuentran divididos en las historias de estos libros, y todos se explican más adelante.

took the top off – *take off;*

pull it down – *pull down;*

blow your house down – *blow down;*

ate the pig up – *eat up;*

tied them up – *tie up;*

see him back – *see back;*

put it back – *put back;*

pulled the covers down – *pull down;*

put it down / put the lid tight down – *put down;*

threw herself down – *throw down;*

keep Beauty from – keep from;

took the lid off – take off;

take her off (to market) – take off – (take away);

carried her off – carry off – (carry away);

have any power over (him) – have power over;

the path led straight up to the door – lead up to;

the music put them both to sleep – put to sleep;

led straight across – lead across;

think it over – think over;

send her away – send away;

take anything away – take away;

ate it all up – eat up.

Este ejemplo más complejo utiliza dos verbos compuestos al mismo tiempo:

he ran in and across the kitchen – corrió dentro y a través de la cocina.

Aún más confusos son los siguientes ejemplos, también de los cuentos de hadas, pues invierten el orden normal de las palabras para dar énfasis:

out she jumped – jump out;

and away they went – go away;

on and on he ran – run on AND run on.

E.2 Verbos compuestos en estas historias

La siguiente es una lista de todos los verbos compuestos que puedes encontrar en las historias de este libro. Es muy probable que haya obviado uno o dos, por lo que pido disculpas.

Los verbos compuestos están más o menos ordenados de acuerdo con la segunda (o tercera) palabra de la frase, ordenadas según las segundas palabras más comunes.

E.2.1 «Up and down»

go up – subir – lejos del observador;

go down – bajar – lejos del observador;

come up – subir – hacia el observador;

come down – bajar – hacia el observador.

Cuando se usa direccionalmente, se puede agregar «*up*» y «*down*» a casi cualquier verbo de movimiento, esto es muy similar en el castellano.

climb up – trepar;

climb down – descender;

look up – mirar arriba;

look down – mirar abajo;

the wolf went slipping and scrabbling down the chimney – El lobo bajó por la chimenea, resbalando y arrastrándose.

Victoria ran up the hill – Victoria subió corriendo la colina;

tears ran down her cheeks – unas lágrimas corrían por sus mejillas.

Las cosas también se pueden mover en diferentes direcciones:

Victoria pulled the bed covers down – Victoria bajó las sábanas / Victoria tiró las sábanas hacia abajo;

Victoria pulled the blankets up – Victoria levantó las mantas / Victoria tiró las mantas por arriba.

Pero ten en cuenta que aquí «*down*» significa desde la cabecera de la cama hasta la pata de la cama, por lo que no es literalmente «*down*». Lo mismo ocurre con «*up*».

El verbo «*draw*», que traducido es «dibujar», también puede significar «tirar».

he drew the sheets up under his chin –se subió las sábanas debajo de la barbilla.

La frase «*throw down*» normalmente significa «lanzar por abajo»:

Victoria threw herself down on the floor – Victoria se tiró al suelo.

Ten en cuenta que en el uso normal «*throw up*» casi siempre significa «vomitar».

Las frases «*to sit up*» y «*to sit down*» tienen diferentes significados:

Victoria sat down – Victoria se sentó;

Victoria sat up – Victoria se enderezó (mientras estaba sentada).

Lo opuesto a «*to sit down*» normalmente sería «*to stand up*» o «*to get up*».

Victoria stood up – Victoria se puso de pie.

Las frases «*get up*» y «*get down*» pueden significar «subir» y «bajar», especialmente si van seguidas de otra preposición.

Victoria got up on the stage – Victoria se subió al escenario;

David got down off his horse – David se bajó de su caballo.

Sin embargo, «*to get up*» a menudo significa «levantar», pero generalmente significa «levantarse».

Victoria got up from the floor (after falling down) – Victoria se levantó del suelo (después de caerse);

Victoria got up late today – Victoria se levantó tarde hoy.

antes de «*getting up*» uno normalmente «*wakes up*»;

Victoria woke up late today – Victoria se despertó tarde hoy.

Las siguientes frases están relacionadas sólo vagamente con el significado de «*down*»:

Victoria lay down in bed – Victoria se acostó en la cama.

Por el contrario, «*lay up*» tiene significados específicos y rara vez se utiliza como «almacenar para el futuro» o «poner un barco en un muelle por un período de tiempo».

Victoria snuggled down in the bed – Victoria se acurrucó en la cama.

Comparar con:

Victoria snuggled up to David – Victoria se acurrucó junto a David.

La frase «*blow down*» normalmente significa «derribar con aire»:

the wolf blew the house down with a single breath – el lobo derribó la casa con un solo soplo.

Sin embargo, «*blow up*» puede significar «llenar con aire» o, más habitualmente, «explotar».

Victoria blew up the balloon – Victoria infló el globo;

David blew up the house – David hizo explotar la casa.

La frase «*put down*» generalmente significa «colocar sobre una superficie» y puede traducirse como «poner», «dejar» o «bajar».

Victoria put down the keys on the table – Victoria dejó las llaves sobre la mesa.

Pero «*put down*» también puede significar «'hablar mal de», «anotar», «insultar» o incluso «sacrificar a un animal enfermo como un acto de misericordia».

«*Put up*» no es lo contrario de «*put down*», y puede significar «colgar», «subir», «levantar» u «hospedar».

El verbo «*pick*» normalmente significa «coger», «recoger», «recolectar», «escoger» o «elegir», y no suele significar «picar».

David picked a flower – David recogió una flor;

Victoria picked a dress – Victoria eligió un vestido.

«*Pick up*» normalmente significa «levantar de una superficie», algo pequeño, usando sólo una mano.

Victoria picked up the keys – Victoria recogió las llaves.

«*Pick up*» también puede significar «levantar».

«*Take up*» normalmente se refiere a un movimiento con las dos manos de un objeto más grande.

Victoria took up the baby in her arms – Victoria tomó al bebé en sus brazos;

his wife took up the hen –su esposa tomó la gallina.

«*Take up*» también puede significar «comenzar», «aceptar» u «ocupar» en casos específicos.

Los siguientes ejemplos están relacionados sólo vagamente con «*up*»:

Victoria dug up some potatoes – Victoria desenterró unas papas;

Jack tied them up in his handkerchief – Jack los ató en su pañuelo;

David made up his bed – David hizo su cama.

«*Make up*» también puede significar «compensar» o «reconciliar».

El sustantivo «*makeup*» es «maquillaje», y el verbo asociado es «*to put on makeup*», «*to put makeup on*» o «*to do his/her/their/X's makeup*».

«*Eat up*» y «*drink up*» implican que una acción se completa.

Victoria ate her food – Victoria comió su comida;

Victoria ate her food up – Victoria comió toda su comida.

E.2.2 «*To*»

Un verbo seguido de «*up to*» implica que una actividad fue en una dirección, hacia un punto o límite fijo.

Victoria ran up to the door – Victoria corrió hacia (hasta) la puerta;

David rode up to the house – David cabalgó hasta la casa;

the path led straight up to the door – el camino conducía directamente a (hasta) la puerta;

the beanstalk grew up to the sky – el tallo creció hasta el cielo;

Jack grew up to be a big strong man – Jack creció para ser un hombre grande y fuerte.

En estos cuentos «*to be up to…*» significa «hacer» o «tramar» algo malo.

he is up to something – él está tramando/haciendo algo (malo);

she is up to no good – ella no trama/hace nada bueno.

Pero «*to be up to*» también puede significar «ser capaz de».

David was up to the task – David era capaz de hacer la tarea.

La frase «*get to*» significa llegar a un lugar o límite determinado.

Victoria got to work on time – Victoria llegó a tiempo al trabajo.

La frase «*put to*» generalmente significa provocar que alguien o algo se encuentre en un estado determinado, puede traducirse como «hacer» o «poner».

the music put them both to sleep – la música los puso a dormir a los dos;

David put the baby to bed – David acostó al bebé en la cama.

Los siguientes ejemplos sólo tienen conexiones débiles con «*to*».

Victoria talked to David – Victoria habló con David;

Victoria looked forward to meeting David – Victoria anticipaba/esperaba (con buenos sentimientos) encontrarse con David.

E.2.3 «*Away* y *from*»

«*From*» es una forma opuesta de «*to*», y sólo se encuentra en una frase de estas historias. «*Keep from*» significa «prevenir» o «impedir».

David kept Victoria from doing her work – David impidió que Victoria hiciera su trabajo.

«*Away*» es el opuesto más comúnmente utilizado a «*to*», que generalmente significa en una dirección alejada del observador.

Victoria said «go away» – Victoria dijo «vete»;

and away they went – y ellos se fueron;

David sent him away – David lo despidió;

Victoria drove away – Victoria se alejó con el coche;

David rode away – David cabalgó alejándose;

the wolf trotted away – el lobo se alejó al trote;

do not take anything away – no te lleves nada;

Beauty was taken away from her home – Bella fue sacada / alejada de su casa.

Los siguientes son usos idiosincrásicos de «away».

the doorman turned them away – el portero los rechazó;

his wife worked away in the kitchen – su esposa trabajaba intensamente / trabajaba sin parar / seguía trabajando en la cocina.

E.2.4 «Off»

«Off» generalmente contrasta con «on» (ver E.2.9 a continuación), pero también puede tener el mismo sentido que «away». (Ten en cuenta también que «off» y «of» son palabras muy diferentes).

Victoria got on the train – Victoria se subió al tren (2.4.1);

Victoria got off the train – Victoria se bajó del tren (2.4.2).

Los siguientes son un poco menos obvios:

Victoria got up on the train – Victoria se subió al tren (2.4.3);

Victoria got down off/from the train – Victoria se bajó del tren (2.4.4).

Las frases 2.4.1 y 2.4.2 implican que la entrada al tren y el andén están más o menos al mismo nivel. Las frases 2.4.3 y 2.4.4 implican que hubo un cambio de nivel significativo desde el andén al tren.

La frase «*to get on with*» puede significar «hacer sin demora» «ponerse a», «ser feliz en compañía de» o «llevarse con».

En muchos casos, el uso de «*off*» en un verbo compuesto significa lo mismo que «*away*». Aquí «*off*» puede implicar algo más cercano que «*away*»; «*off*» también puede implicar el comienzo definitivo de una acción.

David went off to market – David se fue al mercado;

the wolf trotted off –el lobo salió trotando;

Victoria started off on her journey – Victoria emprendió su viaje;

the pig ran off to town –el cerdo se fue corriendo a la ciudad;

Jack carried her off – Jack se la llevó;

Jack had to take her off to market – Jack tuvo que llevarla al mercado;

be off with you – aléjate / vete.

«*Set off*» también puede significar lo mismo que «*start off*» y «*start out*», y significa comenzar en una dirección; véase también E.2.6 a continuación:

Victoria set off on her journey – Victoria emprendió su viaje.

Ejemplos direccionales menos obvios de «*off*»:

Victoria took the lid off the pot – Victoria quitó la tapa de la olla;

David pulled the sheets off the bed – David tiró las sábanas de la cama.

La frase «*break off*» puede tener un significado literal:

David broke a twig off the tree – David rompió una rama del árbol.

Pero también puede ser figurado:

Victoria broke off her relationship with David – Victoria rompió su relación con David.

La frase «*put off*» tiene el significado específico de desalentar o desanimar, y no es lo opuesto a «*put on*», ver E.2.9 a continuación.

Victoria put David off with her bad behaviour – Victoria desanimó a David con su mal comportamiento.

E.2.5 «*Forward*»

La palabra «*forward*» sólo se usa de una manera no obvia en estos cuentos:

look forward (to) – anticipar (con buenos sentimientos);

he was looking forward to having bacon for breakfast – estaba deseando desayunar tocino.

E.2.6 «*Out*»

En un verbo compuesto, «*out*» también puede significar «fuera», pero generalmente significa «salir». Lo opuesto a «*out*» puede ser «*back*» o «*in*».

Como en otros casos, «*go*» implica un movimiento que se aleja del observador y «*come*» implica un movimiento hacia el observador.

Victoria went out of the house (leaving me inside) – Victoria salió de la casa (dejándome adentro);

David came out of the house (and met me in the garden) – David salió de la casa (y me encontró en el jardín);

the wolf crept out of the house – el lobo salió sigilosamente de la casa.

Beauty and the Beast

La frase «*start out*» puede tener dos significados:

Jack started out on his journey – Jack comenzó su viaje;

the giant started out of sleep – el gigante salió del sueño / el gigante se asustó del sueño.

La palabra «*set*» puede significar una colección de cosas que coinciden o que algo está fijo:

a set of cutlery – una colección de cubiertos (del mismo estilo);

the poles were set in concrete – los postes se fijaron en hormigón.

Pero «*set out*» puede significar iniciar un viaje:

David set out on his way home – David emprendió el camino a casa.

«*Set out*» también puede significar «disponer», «colocar» o «arreglar».

Victoria set the things out on the table – Victoria dispuso las cosas sobre la mesa.

Otros ejemplos direccionales:

Victoria stepped out of the house – Victoria salió de la casa (con pasos);

Goldilocks jumped out of the window – Ricitos de Oro saltó por la ventana;

the pig leaped out of the window – el cerdo saltó por la ventana;

David leaned out of the window – David se asomó a la ventana;

Ejemplos direccionales menos obvios:

David got out of the house – David salió de la casa;

the beast got out a bit of bread and cheese for him – la bestia sacó un poco de pan y queso para él;

his wife brought out his harp –su esposa sacó su arpa;

the man pulled out some beans from his pocket – el hombre sacó unos frijoles de su bolsillo;

the man drew out some beans from his pocket – el hombre sacó unos frijoles de su bolsillo.

Significados menos obvios:

Victoria slipped out of the house – Victoria salió de la casa sin ser vista;

Victoria slipped out of her clothes – Victoria se quitó la ropa;

David stretched out on the bed – David se tendió en la cama;

David put the rubbish out – David sacó la basura;

Victoria put the lights out – Victoria apagó las luces;

David laughed out loud – David se rio a carcajadas.

E.2.7 «*Back*»

En un verbo compuesto, «*back*» generalmente significa algún tipo de regreso, hacer algo en dirección opuesta a una acción anterior. Esto significa que puede ser lo contrario a «*out*» o «*away*».

En los verbos compuestos, «*back*» también puede significar regresar a un estado anterior, con un significado de tiempo en lugar de uno direccional.

La palabra «*back*» se puede usar con muchos otros verbos de movimiento. Nuevamente, «*go*» implica un movimiento que se aleja del observador y «*come*» implica un movimiento hacia el observador.

Victoria went back home (and left me alone) – Victoria volvió a casa (y me dejó solo);

David came back home (and cooked food for us) – David volvió a casa (y cocinó para nosotros);

Jack crept back through the kitchen – Jack volvió sigilosamente a través de la cocina;

«*Get back*» muestra el movimiento de regreso a una posición o estado anterior:

get back home! – ¡vuelve a casa!

get back in line – vuelve a la cola / vuelve a tu lugar en la cola.

De manera similar, «*back*» a menudo se usa con objetos para mostrar que las cosas regresan a su posición o estado anterior.

Jack put the harp back in the place he found it – Jack volvió a poner el arpa en el lugar donde la encontró;

Jack's mother was surprised to see him back from market so soon – La madre de Jack se sorprendió al verlo regresar del mercado tan pronto;

you will find yourself back in the castle again –te encontrarás de nuevo en el castillo;

Beauty wished herself back in the castle – Bella deseaba volver al castillo;

Jack took the beans back to the man he met on the road – Jack le devolvió los frijoles al hombre que encontró en el camino;

after a while their hard hearts grew soft and the stone melted back to flesh again –después de un tiempo, sus corazones duros se ablandaron y la piedra volvió a fundirse en carne.

E.2.8 «*In*»

En un verbo compuesto, «*in*» suele tener el significado sencillo de «entrar», pero también puede significar entrar en un estado.

Jack ran in to the kitchen – Jack entró en la cocina corriendo;

David went in to the house (and left me outside) – David entró a la casa (y me dejó afuera);

Victoria came in to the house (and sat down next to us) – Victoria entró a la casa (y se sentó a nuestro lado);

go in peace! – ¡ve en paz!

E.2.9 «*On*»

La palabra «*on*» puede significar literalmente «sobre»; sin embargo, también suele denotar el continuar en una determinada dirección o seguir haciendo algo en el tiempo (sin una dirección implícita). También se utiliza como lo opuesto a «*off*», ver E.2.4 arriba, además, tiene muchos significados que no son obvios.

Goldilocks knocked on the door – Ricitos de Oro llamó a la puerta;

Beauty put on her dress – Bella se puso su vestido.

Ten en cuenta que lo contrario es «*take off*».

Beauty took off her dress – Bella se quitó el vestido;

David got on the horse – David se montó en el caballo (David se trepó en el caballo, el caballo estaba quieto);

Victoria rode on the horse – Victoria se montó en el caballo (El caballo se movió llevando a Victoria).

Pero «*get on with*» significa continuar y concentrarse en algo. También puede significar disfrutar de la compañía de alguien.

David got on with his homework – David siguió con su tarea / Dave se ocupó con su tarea.

Pero «*carry on*» puede significar «continuar».

Jack carried the axe on his back – Jack llevaba el hacha en la espalda;

the giant carried on eating his food – el gigante siguió comiendo su comida.

En un verbo compuesto, «*on*» puede denotar un estado emocional relacionado con otra persona.

Beauty had pity on him – Bella tuvo piedad de él;

see what suffering you have brought on me – mira el sufrimiento que me has traído.

Es muy común que «*on*» denote un movimiento continuo en el espacio o una acción continua en el tiempo.

Jack went on walking until he arrived at the castle – Jack siguió caminando hasta llegar al castillo;

the pig trotted on along the road – el cerdo trotó por el camino / El cerdo continuaba trotando por el camino;

on and on he ran – él corrió y corrió sin parar;

David travelled on for three days – David viajó durante tres días / David continuó viajando durante tres días;

Red Riding Hood wandered on picking flowers – Caperucita Roja vagaba recogiendo flores.

La frase «*going on*» significa «sucediendo» o «pasando».

the woodcutter wanted to see all that was going on there – el leñador quería ver todo lo que pasaba allí / El leñador quería ver todo lo que estaba pasando allí.

E.2.10 «*Over / across / through*»

Los verbos compuestos «*over*», «*across*» y «*through*» suelen tener significados espaciales bastante sencillos y similares. Normalmente se traducen como «sobre», «a través» o «entre», pero hay significados idiosincrásicos ocasionales.

E.2.10.1 «Over»

David went over there – David fue allí;

Victoria came over here – Victoria vino aquí;

the wolf crept over the ground – el lobo se arrastró por el suelo;

the ball bounced over the lawn – la pelota rebotó sobre el césped;

somebody has splashed porridge over the table – alguien ha derramado avena sobre la mesa;

Goldilock's golden hair spread all over the pillow – El cabello dorado de Ricitos de Oro esparcido por toda la almohada.

Algunos usos idiosincrásicos podrían ser:

Victoria had to think it over – Victoria tuvo que pensarlo bien / mucho;

Beauty did not have any power over him – Bella no tenía ningún poder sobre él;

David took a long time to get over his illness – David tardó mucho en superar su enfermedad.

E.2.10.2 «Across»

the wolf pulled the curtains across the window – el lobo corrió las cortinas de la ventana;

the path led straight across the garden – el camino conducía directamente a través del jardín;

Jack ran in and across the kitchen – Jack entró y cruzó la cocina, corriendo.

E.2.10.3 «*Through*»

the wolf crept through the bushes – el lobo se arrastró entre los arbustos;

the ball rolled through the flowers – la pelota rodó entre las flores;

the coin slipped through his fingers – la moneda se deslizó entre sus dedos;

the wind blew through the trees – el viento sopló a través de los árboles;

the woodcutter chopped his way through the trees – el leñador cortó su camino a través de los árboles.

Uso idiosincrático:

Victoria got through a lot of work in a short time – Victoria superó mucho trabajo en poco tiempo.

E.2.11 Otros ejemplos

Los siguientes son algunos ejemplos sencillos que quedan de las historias.

Goldilocks knocked at the door – Ricitos de Oro llamó a la puerta;

Beauty looked at the beast – Bella miró a la bestia;

the pig looked around the garden – el cerdo miró alrededor del jardín;

the wolf hunted around until he found the grandmother's bed clothes – el lobo buscó (por todas partes) hasta que encontró la ropa de cama de la abuela.

Los siguientes no son sencillos:

the Beast heard of Beauty's adventures – la Bestia se enteró de las aventuras de Bella;

but they would not hear of this – pero ellos no se enterarían de esto / pero ellos no aceptarán esto;

her sisters heard about Beauty's good luck – sus hermanas se enteraron de la buena suerte de Bella;

Victoria made the car ready – Victoria preparó el coche;

David took his time with his chores – David se tomó su tiempo / David se tardó con sus quehaceres.

F
Palabras - Ordenado por sección

C.1.01	**beauty**	la bella
	fortune	fortuna
	large	grande
	longer	más extenso
	older	más viejo
	things	cosas
	think	piensa
	wrong	equivocado, malo, incorrecto
C.1.02	**necklace**	collar
	rode	montado
	rose	rosa, subido
	should	debo, debe/-es/-emos/-éis/-en
	times	veces, tiempos
	turning	girando
C.1.03	**days**	dias
	hoping	esperando
	suddenly	repentinamente, de repente
	trying	intentando, difícil
C.1.04	**being**	siendo, estando
	hands	manos
	invisible	invisible
	seen	visto

Beauty and the Beast

	slept	dormido
	sounded	sonado
	without	sin
C.1.05	**beast**	bestia
	beauty's	beauty-[su], beauty is/has - de la bella (posesivo), bella es/está/había
	beside	junto a, al lado de
	covered	cubierto
	dearer	más caro, más apreciado
	largest	lo más grande
	meant	querido decir
	miserable	muy triste, miserable
	paths	veredas, caminos, rutas
	shall	debe, puede, que hace - "shall" es un raro auxiliar inglés. Puede indicar el futuro, la posibilidad o, a veces, una fuerte determinación
	surely	seguramente
C.1.06	**alas**	ay, caramba, qué lástima
	either	o, cualquiera de los dos
	life	vida
	promise	promesa, promete
	tear	lágrima, arranca
C.1.07	**beast's**	Beast-[su], Beast is/has - de la bestia (posesivo), bestia es/está/había
	father's	father-[su], father is/has - del padre (posesivo), padre es/está/había
	joy	alegría
	looks	miras, miradas - it looks (like / as if): parece
	marry	casa - de casar, no un edificio
	unless	a no ser que, a menos que
C.1.08	**dearest**	querido, lo más caro, lo más apreciado
	dining	comiendo
	master	maestro, señor, amo
	might	poderio - auxiliar; puede que, es posible que
	opened	abierto
C.1.09	**feared**	temido

Beauty and the Beast

	learn	aprende
	may	puedo que, puedes/-e/-emos/-éis/-en que, "May": 'Mayo'
	sadden	entristece
	tremble	tembla
C.1.10	**move**	mueve
	played	jugado
	pleased	encantado
	whenever	cuando sea
C.1.11	**calling**	llamando, vocación
	love	ama, amor
	often	a menudo, frecuentemente
C.1.13	**became**	se volvido, se convertido en
	drank	bebido
	due	debido a, vence, programado
	finely	finamente
	gets	obtienes
	powder	polvo
	send	envia
	wake	se despierta
	younger	mas joven
C.1.14	**ah**	ah
	dream	sueño
	feel	sente
	realise	darse cuenta
	walked	caminado
C.1.15	**satin**	satín
	tears	lágrimas, arrancas
	wonder	"to wonder": 'fascinar, preguntarse, estar curiosa'
	young	joven
C.1.16	**freed**	liberado
	fro	de un lado a otro
	spite	rencor - "in spite of": 'no obstante'
	voices	voces
C.1.17	**doorway**	puerta, entrada

Beauty and the Beast

	further	más lejos
	married	casado
	stand	esta de pie
	stone	piedra, roca
	used	usado - la frase en inglés "used to" se usa para mostrar el tiempo pasado habitual, normalmente se traduce como 'soler'. "she used to eat fish every Friday": 'ella solía comer pescado todos los viernes',
C.2.01	children	niños
	dearly	apreciadamente
	finer	más fino
	journey	viaje
	mistake	error
	rich	rico
	sea	mar
	ships	barcos
C.2.02	eldest	el mayor
	embroidered	bordado
	expensive	caro
	given	dado
	horse	caballo
	less	menos
	match	empareja, combina, partido, cerilla
	robe	túnica
	selfish	egoísta
	wave	onda, ola, gesto de saludo con la mano
	youngest	lo más joven
C.2.03	city	ciudad
	several	varios, unos, un poco de
	shelter	refugio
	storm	tormenta
C.2.04	arranged	organizado
	dirty	sucio
	food	comida
	kinds	tipos
	meats	carnes

	most	la mayoría, mayor
	rarest	lo más raro
	richest	lo más rico
	soul	alma
	suit	traje, queda bien
	taken	tomado
	undressed	se desvestido, desvestido, desnudo
C.2.05	**chose**	elegido
	easily	fácilmente
	finest	lo más fino
	flowering	floración, floreciente
	kill	mata
	reminded	recordado, hecho acordar
	sight	visión
	winding	serpenteando
C.2.06	**free**	libre
	pity	pena, compadesce
	pleaded	suplicado
C.2.07	**downcast**	abatido
	fainted	desmayado
	lose	pierde
	nearly	casi, por poco
	save	salva, ahorra, guarda, salvo
	urged	urgido
	yet	aún, ya, todavía
C.2.08	**agree**	estar de acuerdo
C.2.09	**dreadful**	terrible, espantoso
	perhaps	quizás
	true	cierto, verdadero
C.2.10	**every**	cada, todo
	raised	elevado
C.2.11	**anxiously**	ansiosamente
C.2.12	**yourself**	tú-mismo
C.2.13	**lead**	dirige, dirigido, plomo
	questions	preguntas

	swallowed	tragado
	weighed	pesado
C.2.14	**sadly**	tristemente
	sobbing	sollozante, llorando
C.2.15	**breath**	respiración
	deserted	abandonado
	early	temprano
	furry	peludo
	gladly	con alegría
	lap	regazo, vuelta, lame
	rough	áspero, rugoso
C.2.16	**alone**	solo
	held	agarrado
	kindness	amabilidad
	ugly	feo
C.2.17	**flesh**	carne
	thousand	mil
	wedding	boda
C.3.01	**afraid**	temeroso
	black	negro
	ebony	ébano
	gift	regalo
	lost	perdido
	merchant	comerciante
	part	parte
	pleasantly	agradablemente
	prosperous	próspero
C.3.02	**bracelet**	pulsera
	fan	abanico, ventilador, fanático, seguidor
	kissed	besado
	shame	lástima, remordimiento, avergonaza
	smiled	sonreído
	velvet	terciopelo
C.3.03	**amazed**	asombrado
	deep	profundo

	discovered	descubrió
	gifts	regalos
	managed	manejado, administrado, logrado
	overtaken	superado
	travelled	viajado
C.3.04	**disturbed**	perturbado, interrumpido
	fruits	frutas
	plates	platos
	served	servido
C.3.05	**air**	aire
	appeared	aparecido
	escape	escapa
	fountains	fuentes
	fruit	fruta
	offered	ofrecido
	plants	plantas
	plucked	arrancado, desplumado, punteado
C.3.06	**die**	muere, dado (jugete)
	disappeared	desaparecido
	horrified	horrorizado
	months	meses
	obliged	obligado
	spare	repuesto, perdona
	spared	perdonado
C.3.07	**chest**	pecho, baúl
	consent	consentimiento, consiente
	heavy	pesado
	hideous	espantoso, horrible, muy feo
	noticed	notada
	possibly	posiblemente
C.3.08	**admire**	admira
C.3.09	**gentle**	amable, suave
	gently	suavemente
	shake	agita
	stay	permanece

Beauty and the Beast

	weeping	llorando
C.3.10	content	contento
	grew	crecido
	heavily	fuertemente, pesadomente
	images	imágenes
	reflected	reflejada
	reflection	reflexión
	sigh	suspiro, suspira
	smile	sonrisa, sonrie
C.3.11	ill	enfermo
	misfortune	desgracia
	serious	grave, serio
C.3.13	envy	envidia
	eyelids	párpados
	goblet	cáliz, copa - de metallo
	planned	planificado
	slumber	duerme, duermevela
C.3.14	bitterly	amargamente
	fault	culpa, defecto, desperfecto, falla
	fountain	fuente
C.3.15	apart	aparte
	really	realmente
C.3.16	form	forma, formulario
	maiden	doncella
	power	poder, energía
	shape	forma
	wicked	malvado
C.3.17	court	corte, tribunal, cancha, pista
	equal	igual
	grand	gran, grande, excelente
	honour	honor
	noblemen	nobles
C.4.01	blue	azul
	bring	trae
	daughters	hijas

Beauty and the Beast

	sky	cielo
	wish	deseo, desea
C.4.02	**daughter**	hija
	front	frente
	pearls	perlas
	sisters	hermanas
	spoke	hablado
	troubled	preocupado
C.4.03	**castle**	castillo
	heart	corazón
	magnificent	magnífico
	night	noche
	poor	pobre
	silent	silencioso, silencio
C.4.04	**delicious**	delicioso
	filled	llenado, lleno
	gardens	jardines
	handsome	guapo, bonito
	laid	extendido
	music	música
	supper	cena
C.4.05	**break**	rompe, pausa, fractura
	bush	arbusto, bosque
	garden	jardín
	ground	suelo
	suffer	sufre
	trouble	problema, problemas, molesta
C.4.06	**begged**	rogado
	help	ayuda, socorro
	prepared	preparado
	return	regreso, regrese, retorno
	satisfied	satisfecho
	scared	asustado
	wife	esposa
C.4.07	**bride**	novia

	brought	traído
	creature	criatura
C.4.08	feast	banquete
C.4.09	believe	cree
	willing	dispuesto
C.4.10	different	diferente
	mirror	espejo
	surprised	sorprendido
C.4.11	pale	pálido
	week	semana
C.4.12	palm	palma, palmera
	ring	anillo
	ruby	rubí
	suffering	sufrimiento
	tonight	esta noche
	wished	deseado
C.4.13	nights	noches
	us	(a) nosotros
C.4.14	stretched	estirado
C.4.15	prince	príncipe
C.4.16	changed	cambiado
	fairy	hada
	spell	hechizo, deletrea
C.4.17	hearts	corazones
	melted	derretido
	statues	estatuas

G

Palabras - Orden Alfabético

admire	admira	C.3.08
afraid	temeroso	C.3.01
agree	estar de acuerdo	C.2.08
ah	ah	C.1.14
air	aire	C.3.05
alas	ay, caramba, qué lástima	C.1.06
alone	solo	C.2.16
amazed	asombrado	C.3.03
anxiously	ansiosamente	C.2.11
apart	aparte	C.3.15
appeared	aparecido	C.3.05
arranged	organizado	C.2.04
beast	bestia	C.1.05
beast's	Beast-[su], Beast is/has - de la bestia (posesivo), bestia es/está/había	C.1.07
beauty	la bella	C.1.01
beauty's	beauty-[su], beauty is/has - de la bella (posesivo), bella es/está/había	C.1.05
became	se volvido, se convertido en	C.1.13
begged	rogado	C.4.06
being	siendo, estando	C.1.04
believe	cree	C.4.09

Beauty and the Beast

beside	junto a, al lado de	C.1.05
bitterly	amargamente	C.3.14
black	negro	C.3.01
blue	azul	C.4.01
bracelet	pulsera	C.3.02
break	rompe, pausa, fractura	C.4.05
breath	respiración	C.2.15
bride	novia	C.4.07
bring	trae	C.4.01
brought	traído	C.4.07
bush	arbusto, bosque	C.4.05
calling	llamando, vocación	C.1.11
castle	castillo	C.4.03
changed	cambiado	C.4.16
chest	pecho, baúl	C.3.07
children	niños	C.2.01
chose	elegido	C.2.05
city	ciudad	C.2.03
consent	consentimiento, consiente	C.3.07
content	contento	C.3.10
court	corte, tribunal, cancha, pista	C.3.17
covered	cubierto	C.1.05
creature	criatura	C.4.07
daughter	hija	C.4.02
daughters	hijas	C.4.01
days	dias	C.1.03
dearer	más caro, más apreciado	C.1.05
dearest	querido, lo más caro, lo más apreciado	C.1.08
dearly	apreciadamente	C.2.01
deep	profundo	C.3.03
delicious	delicioso	C.4.04
deserted	abandonado	C.2.15
die	muere, dado (jugete)	C.3.06
different	diferente	C.4.10
dining	comiendo	C.1.08

dirty	sucio	C.2.04
disappeared	desaparecido	C.3.06
discovered	descubierto	C.3.03
disturbed	perturbado, interrumpido	C.3.04
doorway	puerta, entrada	C.1.17
downcast	abatido	C.2.07
drank	bebido	C.1.13
dreadful	terrible, espantoso	C.2.09
dream	sueño	C.1.14
due	debido a, vence, programado	C.1.13
early	temprano	C.2.15
easily	fácilmente	C.2.05
ebony	ébano	C.3.01
either	o, cualquiera de los dos	C.1.06
eldest	el mayor	C.2.02
embroidered	bordado	C.2.02
envy	envidia	C.3.13
equal	igual	C.3.17
escape	escapa	C.3.05
every	cada, todo	C.2.10
expensive	caro	C.2.02
eyelids	párpados	C.3.13
fainted	desmayado	C.2.07
fairy	hada	C.4.16
fan	abanico, ventilador, fanático, seguidor	C.3.02
father's	father-[su], father is/has - del padre (posesivo), padre es/está/había	C.1.07
fault	culpa, defecto, desperfecto, falla	C.3.14
feared	temido	C.1.09
feast	banquete	C.4.08
feel	sente	C.1.14
filled	llenado, lleno	C.4.04
finely	finamente	C.1.13
finer	más fino	C.2.01
finest	lo más fino	C.2.05
flesh	carne	C.2.17

flowering	floración, floreciente	C.2.05
food	comida	C.2.04
form	forma, formulario	C.3.16
fortune	fortuna	C.1.01
fountain	fuente	C.3.14
fountains	fuentes	C.3.05
free	libre	C.2.06
freed	liberado	C.1.16
fro	de un lado a otro	C.1.16
front	frente	C.4.02
fruit	fruta	C.3.05
fruits	frutas	C.3.04
furry	peludo	C.2.15
further	más lejos	C.1.17
garden	jardín	C.4.05
gardens	jardines	C.4.04
gentle	amable, suave	C.3.09
gently	suavemente	C.3.09
gets	obtienes	C.1.13
gift	regalo	C.3.01
gifts	regalos	C.3.03
given	dado	C.2.02
gladly	con alegría	C.2.15
goblet	cáliz, copa - de metallo	C.3.13
grand	gran, grande, excelente	C.3.17
grew	crecido	C.3.10
ground	suelo	C.4.05
hands	manos	C.1.04
handsome	guapo, bonito	C.4.04
heart	corazón	C.4.03
hearts	corazones	C.4.17
heavily	fuertemente, pesadomente	C.3.10
heavy	pesado	C.3.07
held	agarrado	C.2.16
help	ayuda, socorro	C.4.06

hideous	espantoso, horrible, muy feo	C.3.07
honour	honor	C.3.17
hoping	esperando	C.1.03
horrified	horrorizado	C.3.06
horse	caballo	C.2.02
ill	enfermo	C.3.11
images	imágenes	C.3.10
invisible	invisible	C.1.04
journey	viaje	C.2.01
joy	alegría	C.1.07
kill	mata	C.2.05
kindness	amabilidad	C.2.16
kinds	tipos	C.2.04
kissed	besado	C.3.02
laid	extendido	C.4.04
lap	regazo, vuelta, lame	C.2.15
large	grande	C.1.01
largest	lo más grande	C.1.05
lead	dirige, dirigido, plomo	C.2.13
learn	aprende	C.1.09
less	menos	C.2.02
life	vida	C.1.06
longer	más extenso	C.1.01
looks	miras, miradas - it looks (like / as if): parece	C.1.07
lose	pierde	C.2.07
lost	perdido	C.3.01
love	ama, amor	C.1.11
magnificent	magnífico	C.4.03
maiden	doncella	C.3.16
managed	manejado, administrado, logrado	C.3.03
married	casado	C.1.17
marry	casa - de casar, no un edificio	C.1.07
master	maestro, señor, amo	C.1.08
match	empareja, combina, partido, cerilla	C.2.02
may	puedo que, puedes/-e/-emos/-éis/-en que, "May": 'Mayo'	C.1.09

meant	querido decir	C.1.05
meats	carnes	C.2.04
melted	derretido	C.4.17
merchant	comerciante	C.3.01
might	poderio - auxiliar; puede que, es posible que	C.1.08
mirror	espejo	C.4.10
miserable	muy triste, miserable	C.1.05
misfortune	desgracia	C.3.11
mistake	error	C.2.01
months	meses	C.3.06
most	la mayoría, mayor	C.2.04
move	mueve	C.1.10
music	música	C.4.04
nearly	casi, por poco	C.2.07
necklace	collar	C.1.02
night	noche	C.4.03
nights	noches	C.4.13
noblemen	nobles	C.3.17
noticed	notada	C.3.07
obliged	obligado	C.3.06
offered	ofrecido	C.3.05
often	a menudo, frecuentemente	C.1.11
older	más viejo	C.1.01
opened	abierto	C.1.08
overtaken	superado	C.3.03
pale	pálido	C.4.11
palm	palma, palmera	C.4.12
part	parte	C.3.01
paths	veredas, caminos, rutas	C.1.05
pearls	perlas	C.4.02
perhaps	quizás	C.2.09
pity	pena, compadesce	C.2.06
planned	planificado	C.3.13
plants	plantas	C.3.05
plates	platos	C.3.04

played	jugado	C.1.10
pleaded	suplicado	C.2.06
pleasantly	agradablemente	C.3.01
pleased	encantado	C.1.10
plucked	arrancado, desplumado, punteado	C.3.05
poor	pobre	C.4.03
possibly	posiblemente	C.3.07
powder	polvo	C.1.13
power	poder, energía	C.3.16
prepared	preparado	C.4.06
prince	príncipe	C.4.15
promise	promesa, promete	C.1.06
prosperous	próspero	C.3.01
questions	preguntas	C.2.13
raised	elevado	C.2.10
rarest	lo más raro	C.2.04
realise	darse cuenta	C.1.14
really	realmente	C.3.15
reflected	reflejada	C.3.10
reflection	reflexión	C.3.10
reminded	recordado, hecho acordar	C.2.05
return	regreso, regrese, retorno	C.4.06
rich	rico	C.2.01
richest	lo más rico	C.2.04
ring	anillo	C.4.12
robe	túnica	C.2.02
rode	montado	C.1.02
rose	rosa, subido	C.1.02
rough	áspero, rugoso	C.2.15
ruby	rubí	C.4.12
sadden	entristece	C.1.09
sadly	tristemente	C.2.14
satin	satín	C.1.15
satisfied	satisfecho	C.4.06
save	salva, ahorra, guarda, salvo	C.2.07

Beauty and the Beast

scared	asustado	C.4.06
sea	mar	C.2.01
seen	visto	C.1.04
selfish	egoísta	C.2.02
send	envia	C.1.13
serious	grave, serio	C.3.11
served	servido	C.3.04
several	varios, unos, un poco de	C.2.03
shake	agita	C.3.09
shall	debe, puede, que hace - "shall" es un raro auxiliar inglés. Puede indicar el futuro, la posibilidad o, a veces, una fuerte determinación	C.1.05
shame	lástima, remordimiento, avergonaza	C.3.02
shape	forma	C.3.16
shelter	refugio	C.2.03
ships	barcos	C.2.01
should	debo, debe/-es/-emos/-éis/-en	C.1.02
sigh	suspiro, suspira	C.3.10
sight	visión	C.2.05
silent	silencioso, silencio	C.4.03
sisters	hermanas	C.4.02
sky	cielo	C.4.01
slept	dormido	C.1.04
slumber	duerme, duermevela	C.3.13
smile	sonrisa, sonrie	C.3.10
smiled	sonreído	C.3.02
sobbing	sollozante, llorando	C.2.14
soul	alma	C.2.04
sounded	sonado	C.1.04
spare	repuesto, perdona	C.3.06
spared	perdonado	C.3.06
spell	hechizo, deletrea	C.4.16
spite	rencor - "in spite of": 'no obstante'	C.1.16
spoke	hablado	C.4.02
stand	esta de pie	C.1.17

statues	estatuas	C.4.17
stay	permanece	C.3.09
stone	piedra, roca	C.1.17
storm	tormenta	C.2.03
stretched	estirado	C.4.14
suddenly	repentinamente, de repente	C.1.03
suffer	sufre	C.4.05
suffering	sufrimiento	C.4.12
suit	traje, queda bien	C.2.04
supper	cena	C.4.04
surely	seguramente	C.1.05
surprised	sorprendido	C.4.10
swallowed	tragado	C.2.13
taken	tomado	C.2.04
tear	lágrima, arranca	C.1.06
tears	lágrimas, arrancas	C.1.15
things	cosas	C.1.01
think	piensa	C.1.01
thousand	mil	C.2.17
times	veces, tiempos	C.1.02
tonight	esta noche	C.4.12
travelled	viajado	C.3.03
tremble	tembla	C.1.09
trouble	problema, problemas, molesta	C.4.05
troubled	preocupado	C.4.02
true	cierto, verdadero	C.2.09
trying	intentando, difícil	C.1.03
turning	girando	C.1.02
ugly	feo	C.2.16
undressed	se desvestido, desvestido, desnudo	C.2.04
unless	a no ser que, a menos que	C.1.07
urged	urgido	C.2.07
us	(a) nosotros	C.4.13

Beauty and the Beast

used	usado - la frase en inglés "used to" se usa para mostrar el tiempo pasado habitual, normalmente se traduce como 'soler'. "she used to eat fish every Friday": 'ella solía comer pescado todos los viernes',	C.1.17
velvet	terciopelo	C.3.02
voices	voces	C.1.16
wake	se despierta	C.1.13
walked	caminado	C.1.14
wave	onda, ola, gesto de saludo con la mano	C.2.02
wedding	boda	C.2.17
week	semana	C.4.11
weeping	llorando	C.3.09
weighed	pesado	C.2.13
whenever	cuando sea	C.1.10
wicked	malvado	C.3.16
wife	esposa	C.4.06
willing	dispuesto	C.4.09
winding	serpenteando	C.2.05
wish	deseo, desea	C.4.01
wished	deseado	C.4.12
without	sin	C.1.04
wonder	"to wonder": 'fascinar, preguntarse, estar curiosa'	C.1.15
wrong	equivocado, malo, incorrecto	C.1.01
yet	aún, ya, todavía	C.2.07
young	joven	C.1.15
younger	mas joven	C.1.13
youngest	lo más joven	C.2.02
yourself	tú-mismo	C.2.12